THE STILLNESS OF THE WORLD
BEFORE BACH

Fiction by Lars Gustafsson

The Death of a Beekeeper
(Translated by Janet K. Swaffar
and Guntram H. Weber)

The Tennis Players
(Translated by Yvonne L. Sandstroem)

Sigismund
(Translated by John Weinstock)

Stories of Happy People
(Translated by Yvonne L. Sandstroem
and John Weinstock)

Funeral Music for Freemasons
(Translated by Yvonne L. Sandstroem)

LARS GUSTAFSSON

THE STILLNESS OF THE WORLD BEFORE BACH

NEW SELECTED POEMS

Edited by Christopher Middleton

Translations by Robin Fulton, Philip Martin,
Yvonne L. Sandstroem, Harriett Watts, and
Christopher Middleton in collaboration with
Lars Gustafsson

A NEW DIRECTIONS BOOK

The translations in this volume are of poems in Swedish originally collected in the following books by Lars Gustafsson: from Norstedts Förlag, *Ballongfararna* (1962), *En förmiddag in Sverige* (1963), *En resa till jordens medelpunkt* (1966), *Broderna Wright uppsoker Kitty Hawk* (1968), *Varma rum och kalla* (1972), *Sonetter* (1977), *Artesiska brunnar cartesianska drömmar* (1980), *Ur bild i bild—Samlade dikter 1950–1980* (1982), *Världens tystnad före Bach* (1983), and *Fåglarna* (1984); from Albert Bonniers Förlag, *Kärleksförklaring till en sefardisk dam* (1970).

Manufactured in the United States of America
First published clothbound and as New Directions Paperback 656 in 1988
Published simultaneously in Canada by Penguin Books Canada Limited

Library of Congress Cataloging-in-Publication Data

Gustafsson, Lars, 1936-
     [Poems. English. Selections]
     The stillness of the world before Bach: new selected poems / Lars Gustafsson; edited by Christopher Middleton; translations by Robin Fulton . . . [et al.] in collaboration with Lars Gustafsson.
          p.   cm.
     1. Gustafsson, Lars, 1936–   —Translations, English.
I. Middleton, Christopher.   II. Title.
PT9876.17.U8A24 1988
839.7'174—dc 19   87-31669
                                                                                        CIP

New Directions Books are published for James Laughlin
by New Directions Publishing Corporation,
80 Eighth Avenue, New York 10011

Contents

from *Declaration of Love to a Sephardic Lady* / *Kärleksförklaring till en sefardisk dam* (1970)

from *Warm Rooms and Cold* / *Varma rum och kalla* (1972)

from *Sonnets* / *Sonetter* (1977)

from *Artesian Wells Cartesian Dreams* / *Artesiska brunnar cartesianska drömmar* (1980)

Editorial Note

The translations I've selected come from the following sources: *Selected Poems,* translated by Robin Fulton (New York: New Rivers Press, 1972); *Delos,* 6, 1971, in which Harriett Watts's translations appeared; *Warm Rooms and Cold,* translated by Yvonne L. Sandstroem (Providence: Copper Beach Press, 1975); *Quarterly Review of Literature,* XXIII, Poetry Series IV, edited by T. and R. Weiss, 1982, with Philip Martin's translations.

Yvonne L. Sandstroem's translations of "Sonnet I" and the sestinas appeared in *Scandinavian Literature in a Transcultural Context: Papers from the XVth IASS Conference,* University of Washington, 1984. Her translation of "Elegy on a Dead Labrador" was first published in *The New Yorker.* All my translations were made in close collaboration with Lars Gustafsson, since I do not know Swedish; some of them have been previously published in *Northern Literary Quarterly* and *Southern Humanities Review;* "Border Zone, Minefield, Snow East of Bebra" and "Notes on the 1860s" first appeared in *The New Yorker.*

Translators' initials appear in the contents and also follow under each translation in the text.

C.M.

Introduction

Lars Gustafsson arrived as a writer during the early-to-mid-1960s, when his poems, novels, and essays began to be translated, first into German, subsequently into other European languages. During the next decade he was invited to international congresses; his role as an editor (*Bonniers Literary Magazine*) brought him into contact with many eminent minds and into the thick of ideological and philosophical conflicts of that time. For good reason his poems were translated first (by Hans Magnus Enzensberger): he has remained distinctively a poet, insofar as his novels and essays usually combine exploratory and fabulous features with keen observation, a fascination with character in conflict as the subjective (or existential) axis of history, and a delight in story for its own complex or simple sake. As is sometimes the case with poets, too, he has a native landscape, Västmanlands Län in Sweden, which figures in many of his poems and is progressively reinvented in several of his novels—Christopher Polhem, builder of the winch at Blankstöten, is one of these inventions, another is the Mal monster who dwells in the icy deeps of a real lake and once bit through an iron chain lowered to detect whether or not he (or she) was there. For myself, too, I find continuously in Gustafsson's poems, as a presence no less real than Swedish words, a Swedish light, with pearly atmospheres, or quite transparent.

Through the extraordinary thematic complexity of Gustafsson's writings runs a philosophic thread. He studied philosophy at Uppsala (1955–56 and 1958) and at Oxford (1957) under Gilbert Ryle. His treatise on philosophies of language, *Språk och lögn* ("Language and Lie"), appeared in 1978: this was a critique of mimetic or "representational" views of language in Nietzsche, Alexander Bryan Johnson, and Fritz Mauthner, and Gustafsson argued in favor of a transitive (also actually much more ancient) theory in which language procures forms for intelligence rather than rendering contents of experience. Yet philosophizing is the tone rather than the substance of his poems. Certainly his "philosophy" is anything but a set of axioms through which to interpret the world. In fact, the contrary is the case. From Husserl's later phenomenology, by his own account, Gustafsson drew the lesson that the world needs to be seen afresh, without being intercepted by interpretations. Things aren't identical with the views in which we clothe them. As regards his poetics, this meant that, early on, he branched away from the Swedish modernist predilection for seeing (and interpreting) a thing in terms of something else, thus metaphorically. His own predilection was to see the naked thing in its secrecy, its otherness, or to invent imaginary things, whereby the whole poem, moving through signs in juxtaposition, tends to become a parable.

Each poem accordingly, as his work matured, became an experiment in thinking. The air or tone of the poem might well be that of a voice philosophizing, but that voice's radically conjectural style tests the limits of thought (within the conceptual field devised for experiment). The voice may also penetrate such limits and arrive, beyond any grief of thought, at surprise, revelation, the unknown. To this extent Gustafsson was also branching decisively away from the elegiac pathos which, again by his own account, had hitherto regulated Swedish poems and drained from them the signs of active pleasure in the world. His own work over the last ten years has enthroned the pleasure principle in Swedish poetry, and it includes in its large sensory and imaginative scope not only the impulse of questioning, but also a glow of emotion exhilarated, a fine and breezy feeling. He is no more a philosophical poet than Jorge Luis Borges is a philosophical storyteller.

Reading Gustafsson, one is tempted to sit up very straight in view of his amazing erudition. His range is that of a much-traveled, many-minded novelist, perhaps. The erudition is apparent in his poems, but they carry it, all things considered, very lightly. A word about this would not be out of place. He is familiar with half a dozen languages and literatures other than Swedish. Conflating alphabetically (from poems and novels alone) his areas of real knowledge, I arrived at the following minimum catalog: acoustics, aeronautics, animal psychology, architecture, ballet, ballooning, beekeeping, climatology, computer science, cooking, earth science, esoterica (e.g., Gnosticism, and the ten Sephiroth of the Kabbalah are concealed in "Canal Landscape with Ten Locks"), information theory, linguistics, mathematics, music, ornithology, painting, philosophy, physics, politics, several specific but heterogeneous cultural landscapes, sexuality, submarines, tennis, and utopias. With each new novel the field expands, and his novels and poems till now also have tended to dovetail thematically (a novel is a house, he says, a poem is a man running down a corridor in it). This massive erudition has to be seen for what it is: the mobile cognitive surface of a mind restlessly reinventing itself, imagining depths of peace and depths of conflict as neighboring regions in any single existential act. It is a mind imaginatively exploring worlds unknown, or still hidden—"secret pockets in space, time and being," he calls them. It is a mind, too, which is passionately and morally concerned for the globe, its history, its future. The surface is no mere display, no shallow glitter. It shudders and develops with the cut and thrust of forces (commonly called "ideas") surging from below.

To generalize as I must, so as not to intercept the poems themselves: the objects of this erudition are phenomenal complexes which allow Lars Gustafsson's imagination free play ("ludic elasticity") and a sharpening of referential focus. And the philosophical air is the style itself of language inventing its objects as it advances toward them. The instigator of the poem, poet or reader, will not trap objects in concept or habit, but will always allow for unpredictable shifts of perspective upon the shifting relative positions of the phenomena in their fields. From this mobility derives the factor of surprise in the poem, not to mention the transparency, the lucidity. The momentum of "lyrical enthusiasm" is not thwarted, it is lightened by the philosophical air. Notably after the mid-1970s (Gustafsson has passed through several decisive "periods"), the poems as delicately suspended experiments in thinking are launched, with personality but beyond it, to glide in a free fall, guided by wonder rather than any excogitated plan, in what he calls the "Well" of the cosmos, the space-time tunnel through which all being travels. The poem, then, is a kind of "glide" to the pulse of a sensibility uncramped by local fidget. The pull of thought itself, as thought expands, fills "secret pockets" in those times and spaces where the word comes to life. Gustafsson thus argues that the poem exists much as a mathematical theorem does: as the theorem waits to be formulated, the poem waits for the poet to discover it. The foregoing metaphor of gliding expectancy is invertible: the psyche, thinking or thoughtless, contains, if anything, layers of reality that wait. They are waiting for a style to surprise them, so that they may be spoken.

The selecting of translations was done in three stages, and at each stage the poet was consulted. First he and I made (1985–86) some translations of poems he had chosen, largely from *Fåglarna* ("Birds," 1984), and we continued with poems from earlier books until we had about thirty translations. From among these I chose only those texts which seemed to work best in English. Next I combed existing translations (see Editorial Note) and preferred those which seemed most distinctive in themselves, as poems, and most sensitive to the qualities of early, middle, and later Gustafsson. I did not try to close gaps, if any, by choosing from the comprehensive 1981 collection *Ur bild i bild—Samlade dikter 1950–80* poems which might be important but had not been translated: we already had ample material for a book of the desired size. In addition, I did not question the fidelity of the translations by now chosen; after all, the other translators knew Swedish and I did not. Nor, in reading those translations, had I detected any passages hinting at possible error. Philip Martin's translations might, here and there, deviate minutely from their originals; but Martin has described (*QRL,* Poetry Series IV, 1982, p. 6) how, when his versions were being worked out in consultation with Gustafsson, deviations in the English occasionally led to changes in the original. At the third stage, I solicited from the other translators their second thoughts—and there were a few, so wording was revised here and there and typographical errors were corrected. Some other poems might have been translated if Lars Gustafsson had preferred to start from scratch and limit the selection to his own choice of originals; even then, the result would, I believe, have overlapped in large measure with what we now have. I am most grateful to Robin Fulton, Philip Martin, Yvonne L. Sandstroem, and Harriett Watts for their trust and help, and to Lars Gustafsson for his patience—in English and German—during our hours of work together.

Christopher Middleton

After Rain

The sky of summer rain, like an X-ray film:
all glimmers and vague shadows.
The forest still, and not a single bird.
Your own eye like a spilt drop under the clouds,
reflecting the world: glimmers and vague shadows.
And suddenly you see who you are:
perplexed stranger between mind and clouds,
with only the membrane of an image holding
the world's depths and the eye's darkness apart.

[P.M.]

stronger than the trees,
t to like me,
it you ... me I'll tell you about the Hague.

In the Hague there are long streets,
tree by tree and the light falls straight.
In the Hague you're only a little girl,
you run quickly and the wind whistles,

you're so eager, you're rushing somewhere
and you don't see that the long shadow falls.
In the Hague there are many bridges and lanes
and the laughter of the girls is like a swarm of birds,

you hear them and hurry on, for nuns it's Sunday,
and the houses stand white and high and somewhere
by a forgotten canal there is a bridge
and at the bridge a stone and in the stone a crack.

You're running through the Hague after something,
and the streets are long, you lean against the wind,
and the laughter of the girls and you're looking for a crack,
but the stone is smooth and doesn't open.

All the bells in the Hague are striking now,
and it's the whitest Sunday, you don't
find your way and no bridge is the right one,
and you're searching for something that frightened you,

and the wind and the light and Sunday.
By a forgotten canal by a bridge, someone
stands turned away with his back to you.
Don't be frightened, he's waiting, in the Hague.

[R.F.]

Fire and Air Machine

An antiquated device—
driven by fire and air,
the separate parts so ingeniously
assembled, that even the water,
there, far beneath you, the deep water,
far beneath everything seen,
becomes, to some measure, tangible.

It has also been called: air machine,
and in it one may venture
ascents, a single trip at least,
as the fiery air, the hot steam
gradually cools and evaporates,
while the machine is climbing from zero
up to those heights

where the winter to come is forming.
And from that point, there's no return.
Its mechanism will also allow,
with help from the fire and the air, a short-term
chance to retrieve and relive days from the past.
Summer, more ancient than your restlessness, your name.
It operates slowly, with a muffled sound.

What do you see there?
Its construction doesn't allow you to see things.

[H.W.]

The Balloonists

Look at the man there in the top hat.
He's leaning out and looking to the west.
It's early morning, echoing light.

The city waits in the distance with its bells,
the spires cast their blue and harmless shadows.
It's very calm, it's almost time to leave.

Close up, the balloon looks huge, a giant pumpkin
growing and glowing, many-colored.
And the noise from the crowd: like a swarm of bumblebees.

They're waving and shouting to the travelers in the basket,
who pretend not to notice and won't name their destination.
They're quite still, they're ready for the voyage.

The man in the top hat is still observing
and now he lifts a tube of shining brass
to look for clouds perhaps or something invisible.

When they ascend they'll dwindle to a speck
till when they reach the highest strata, snow,
the very whitest snow, chilling and blinding,

will fill the air they breathe and touch their foreheads.
In autumn you can see it fall like frost,
breath from the heights groping about the fields,

and some autumn when the frost comes early
you'll suddenly recall them and their flight,
and picture them still rising, dizzily higher

through an air thinner than the air of winter
with a sound like that of splintering glass
from dense woods of brittle rain

and how they rise still higher through the years
till even the memory sings as brittle as glass.
But that's unbearable, so don't believe me!

It's a pleasure trip, an adventure for connoisseurs!
A gentleman in morning dress and bright-blue waistcoat
slowly signals with a white-gloved hand.

It's free, it's already rising,
little by little the cheering fades below.

[P.M.]

Summer Song

Once there were some birds in a meadow
who rose like a cloud and disappeared.

Summer, with grass and herbs abounding,
it's still there, and with softer wing beats,

someone finds its place: it's here, only here.
Bees humming in the leaves, the shortest waves

beating lively against the shore,
sticks and leaves, lightest rushes

dried by winters, over and over,
they've always been here, and death itself

won't carry them off; the whitest clouds roll,
the biggest, the quietest clouds over sticks and leaves.

An old stone quarry
abandoned in high, sparse wood,

a place of ferns and heavy boulders;
the whitest dust has settled long ago,

the heavy boom of the wheels has gone too.

Thus freedom exists, it does
only here, at the center, yes it does exist.

And the heart beating faster.

"This is my eye, I'll lend it to you."
Sticks and leaves, over and over again,

you collect them easily in one hand
until a breeze carries them off again.

Off, as if to other lands, where there was safety
just a while ago, where nothing can be reached anymore.

And summer, grass in hand, existed,
as clearly as a needle in the eye exists.

Lost in that wood where light and shadows go.
The old sound grew, and its strength

suddenly seized from days, and months, and years:
the things that keep things up.

"Still further in among the trees your voice."
One sound can overshadow another.

Sticks and straws, sticks and leaves,
over and over again: the solar plexus

has an insignificant nerve that tells us our direction,
and when the light rises it can tell us where we are,

but it leaves us in doubt when night comes.
We exist, but only here at the center, yes we do

but only here in the summer, it's here, only here,
and we rose like a cloud and disappeared

but didn't know it ourselves. "Here's my eye,
I'll lend it to you, but only to make you see."

Once there were some birds in a meadow
who rose like a cloud and disappeared.

                                        [Y.L.S.]

In Time

One of the pictures shows a sleeper,
yes someone sleeping, with a sleeper's face,
where the features are smoothed down and the heart's at ease.

He is sleeping in high grass, its shadows sway,
this is one who is inside time, so far in
that he sleeps in grass and is at peace in its shadow.

In the background the landscape billows gently: a swell,
it is sleeping in another sleep with the same breath.
And in the shadow close by stands a huge panther,

solitary, most still of all, awake.
It is waiting for the sleeper, with its heart taut,
and he who is sleeping is waiting for the leap.

It will come when he wakens,
it will come only if he wakens

[R.F.]

Beyond Irony

Rising sunlight and falling sound,
towards afternoon a duller world, as in sleep.

When a window is open far from here
a dizzying light wavers through the room

and touches its walls, one by one.

On days I am not here the same happens,
but unwatched: the whole world is unwatched.

The light sneaks artfully through the branches,
and the bird sings his little ballad unseen by me,

it rises when it wants to and vanishes.
There is restlessness here, but not despair.

[R.F.]

The Conditions

There were two yellow houses which blocked the view.
But a road could be seen behind, green slope,

distance, calmness so far the air trembled.
And suddenly people were there, in red sweaters.

They went past so quickly they were forgotten,
but returned like a fragment out of a contest

whose end and beginning were both hopelessly hidden.

Cyclists in an obscure part of the race, without context,
so that the first could be the last or vice versa.

They can only exist so long as they are not hidden.

Then there was a train that passed with all the windows open
through summer: a stronger memory, a stronger time.

What an open landscape, roads, waving hands!

And when I looked up from the book all the windows were dark,
with the curtains fluttering inwards in a mute draft.

I looked and I looked. It could have been eternal.
I understood that of such stuff all days are made.

[R.F.]

The Fortress

In a milder region it was autumn. But we journeyed across very desolate waters. Solemn swell, mist, everything solemn, and high steamer hulls went in procession on the horizon, all the time in the same direction. They wanted away.

Furthest out in the loneliness we found an island. The ground was white with a light frost: we were frozen. At the jetty there were high barracks, with crumbling plaster, the soldiers had peculiar baggy uniforms with fringes. They did not see us. Then it became quieter, more and more desolate the further away we went.

Quite soon you will discover that large parts of the island are built up, it is full of holes like a honeycomb and at times there is an underground echoing beneath our feet. Endless galleries, passageways, casemates with stalactites in the roof, frost-covered mounds of earth which from underneath are echoing vaults, where the water drips. Tumbled bricks, passages where you must crouch, monotonous sound of water breaking on the shore. We are nearer now. Through a gap the sea is visible. Everywhere has fallen into ruins, thick iron clamps struggle in vain against bulging walls. Steep stairways for the hurrying tramp of boots, but abandoned, cavities, hiding places. Dusk is coming.

At last we reached the final crest, the furthest, and could see the most remarkable part of all.

These are the big cannons. They are more immense than any you have ever seen, completely boundless in their weight, their maniacal immensity. They rest heavily on their colossal carriages, enormous cogwheels for directing them have forever rusted fast into each other. The lifts for the ammunition, almost unrecognizable with rust, prove the vast dimensions. Ten, eleven, twelve—how many can they be? A defiant row which is still pointing out over the water.

They stand waiting for something huge that will come, the absence of an unimaginable roar hangs over the water. They are abandoned, the last who wait. Perhaps he took another way?

Then we look back into the island. Everywhere these huge endeavors, these galleries and passageways which are slowly collapsing. And the big cannons.

Although we have forgotten it, we must have been here before, once, many times.

[R.F.]

The Dog

"Home to a calmer country."
There is no country calmer than this.

It was sunny and I walked across the ice,
the great open ice swept clean by wind,

and it was Sunday. Then I saw something peculiar,
a little black dog, quite on its own,

running as hard as it could, straight as an arrow,
away from land, out towards the open

where everything vanished like mist at the horizon.
It ran very fast, not looking to left or right,

like a black ball of wool which the wind caught
and bowled across the gleaming blue.

I stood for a long time looking after it.
It seemed as if it would never stop. At last it was gone.

There is no country calmer than this.

[P.M.]

Snow

Early, in the light grayness after snowfall
I heard the child murmuring rhymes and halfwords.

It was a language from a stranger's mouth,
lighter than ours, more gentle, falling like snow.

In lovers' faces for a helpless moment
there's a glimpse of something, before they know they love

and change everything back to what it was.
When glass bursts you hear a special sound

and cracks run through frozen lakes,
no bird flies so swiftly.

I cannot count the dawns I've seen, and none
was matched by the day that followed.

It goes by. It doesn't wait. The crack runs.

But in the light gray, the indefinite, there we could live.
You know the look of snow just when it's fallen.

[P.M.]

A Landscape

September.
On the other hill a house is being built,
slowly becoming ready.
Fresh timber can be seen among the aspens.
On a still day the hammer-blows reach here,
and penetrate deeper and deeper into sleep.
The hopeful get up early.

They don't think to look in all directions.

Three days of milk-white mist;
it was persistent
and would not leave the treetops.

There are three paths which start from here:
the first leads down to water,
still, with some island stone.
The second winds through forest badly thinned
and then down to water,
also still, but with more stones.
The third runs deeper into distance,
loses itself in contexts, networks,
in that indefinite thing the learned call *topography,*
hills, railway tunnels, water meadows, forest domains,
which are all, as it were, resumed by these roads
into larger contexts, longer distances,
the topographical labyrinth
which man populates
with fences, railway bridges, branching directions.

Everywhere directions, possibilities,
and only he who stands still
is at the center:

the moment you move
everything imperceptibly turns round,
with you as axle in a mighty wheel:
with every step you take, the mountains also take one.

And when in the eighteenth century
a topographer measured and described this region
he found it worthy of note
that the main part of this parish
lies under water.

Here we often read about the past.
We read about the dead.
But not about the unborn.

Hence the region ought to have two churches:
the white one, where it stands now by the road,
and another, far to the west,
three fathoms under water, for the unborn,
with its own chime of bells heard only in mist:
The September Church Under the Water.

At a place called Djupnäs,
with high white rooms facing the lake
and large, solemn-faced stoves,
swallows flit in and out through the windows,
there it is Sunday and the cows are lowing.

But the same swallows
in winter flock together under the water
to sleep: like a snowfall they descend
to rest on the tower of the other church,
of the September Church

(which is crowned with a copper Fish, no Cock.
At extreme low-water a hundred and fifty years ago
it became visible and struck with a great fear
all those who saw it)

How the day is filled
with a multitude of sounds and promises:
there is life in the topographical labyrinth
and we, we too are living
together with the dead.

The unborn share this labyrinth with us.

Noon.
And the radio on its yellow shelf
becomes confused in its fine circuits,
carelessly mixes Shostakovich and Franz Berwald,
the swallows and some huge thing that's approaching,
through mist, to the sound of a small drum.
Don't you hear? It listens,
the whole landscape's an ear, a huge ear!

In mist all swallows sit still.

The one great undertaking is impossible:
to turn the past about, to step back into it,
change twilight into dawn, set the past right.
When someone dies it's beyond help,
and the tears and screams vanish into time,
and time shuts and the screams remain,
are shut in there
inside the labyrinth.

"And therefore"
said the Misanthrope
(an elderly gentleman in a remote house
further out on the headland: I sail past
and see his shirts fluttering from a line)
after reminding us of sieges and
famines in different directions in different times,
and having in detail described the childhood of industrialism
with four-year-olds shut into mines

till their eyes were extinguished and went dead
simply *extinguished*, the flame turned down
so twilight comes

"and for this reason
humanity cannot evolve
towards happiness"
because no evolution can undo the past.

"There are only days. Only landscapes."

In Trummelsberg, in the west, you can find remains
of a furnace from the fifteenth century.
That place, everyone knows, is hard to find.

The hopeful get up early
and they don't think to look in all directions.

In mist all swallows sit still.
It listens in the topographical labyrinth,
like a huge ear it listens, don't you hear?
The bells of the September Church are ringing,
muffled drums, drums under the water,
three fathoms down:
heard only when air pressure is low.

The unborn share the labyrinth with the born.
And we, we read about the dead.
In all kinds of languages and signs we read.

The unborn, they only listen. Listen.

Like some vast lake which, turned in on itself,
feeds from deep mists
island after island, no directions

and the field-vole's nest, cunningly hidden in the grass,
where the blind newborn are sleeping,
tightly, tightly, hardly bigger than fingertips,
small pink creatures sleeping in the moss
and no one shall discover them,

I say *no one:* they warm each other
and they sleep.

[P.M.]

from A Journey to the Center of the Earth

To the center of the earth.
The ways down change with the seasons,
indeed almost more swiftly at times
wet fields, extinct volcanoes, closed lifts,
one could say: each one his own way down.
Mine lies in a cathedral, "underneath cast-iron vaults."

Further away in the same great autumn under dark smoke
in an odor of sour potato tops and plowed fields
East Europe's cathedrals rise out of the evening mists.

Bucharest, Warsaw, Budapest and Prague
all have cathedrals—as you thought—
forgotten spires, defiant stone, gargoyles,

threadbare with the years, the color flaking, the stone loose,
but existing loftily, with a man at the door

who points upwards: at the holes in the walls
where fat doves fly in and out, clouds of jackdaws

and these high vaults which the handbook advises us to admire.

But under the floors there is something much more interesting.
It is called improperly "catacombs," a lower church,

a way which leads downwards through endless stairways
till the sounds of the street, and of the doves, vanish.

Labyrinths, low vaults with something red on the walls,
an unknown substance which sticks to the finger

and gives an indescribable *biological* impression:
phosphorous from bones of the dead that were piled there.

Did we go along the passages for days or weeks?
Did the air become more and more dense? What pressure

when we thought of the high towers above us!

And further into the darkness, left behind,
piled carefully and close up under the roof,

first all the thigh bones in one vault, all from the Middle Ages,
(when the vault was built, all the plagues and sieges)

all the heads in one, and the same weird gloom

conceals and namelessly confuses these neighbors.

The torch smoked and dripped on the floor.
And I understood we had come right to the end
and stood at the center.

[R.F.]

Bombus Terrestris*

When the air rests the lakes also rest
the large bright lakes still as quicksilver.

The sleeping dogs breathe in ever shorter rhythm.
The lowest sounds of all are felt like tremblings.

And they are held hidden in large organ pipes,
sixteen feet or more, till it is time.

But out of the small holes in the earth the sound comes.

With falling air pressure the sounds of the distant trains are drowned,
they change and move soundlessly between track and track.

A flying man who lives far within the wood
has folded up his wings and sleeps in the rain.

It is not in the beginning and not at the end.
It is the mainland, vast stretches

in the inner part of the map, deep within time,
a forest of years stands sheltering in every direction,

and the larks rise, like a jubilant cloud,
but always some fall down dead, and vanish.

Too warm for freezing, too cold
for living, so far within the world.

Winter in reverse, seasons and year backwards.
When the air rests, the lakes also rest.

* Bombus = bumblebee (Ed.)

But at the lowest height, a handsbreadth above the ground
the temperature distinctly changes; two degrees warmer

and several dull brown sounds.
The whole of natural science is about warmth

and low sheltering clouds.

[R.F.]

The Machines

Some machines came early,
others, late. Outside their own time,
the world doesn't really have room for them.

Heron's fountain, atl-atl, voltaic pile.
The famed mine shaft machinery in Falun. Curiosities:
The "pneumatic corn-sweep"
Una macchina per riscaldare i piedi

The machines that we notice are those
from another century: they seem to be placeless.
They become obvious, take on meaning.

Yet just what they mean, nobody knows.

The hydraulic mine device: an apparatus
with two shafts, which run in opposite directions,
made to convey force out over great distances.
What does the hydraulic mine device mean?

The mines in the Harz anno 1723

The lithograph swarms with people. Men,
as tiny as flies, ride up and down in the baskets.
And next to the foaming waterfall, illustration figure *j*,
"La Grande Machine," which runs all the drive-belts.

It would indeed be conceivable
that steam engine and general-mechanical-instrument,
Heron's fountain and voltaic pile
might all be combined. No one has done it.
Residue of possibilities.

A foreign language that no one has ever spoken.
And, strictly speaking, grammar itself
is another machine,
emitting, from the midst of innumerable sequences,
the mutter of communication:
"instruments of reproduction," the "procreative members"
"outcries," "stifled whispers."

When the words disappear, the grammar remains,
and that's what we call: a machine. Yet what it means,
nobody knows. A foreign language.

A totally foreign language.
A totally foreign language.
A totally foreign language.

The lithograph swarms with people. Words,
as tiny as flies, ride up and down in the baskets,
and next to the foaming waterfall, illustration figure *j*,
"La Grande Machine," which runs all the drive-belts.

                                                    [H.W.]

Discussions

In antiquated manuals of acoustics
bizarre experiments are proposed to us!

Seek out a garden, absolutely symmetrical,
enclosed on all sides by a wall
(with right-angled corners)
and having gone to the remotest corner
fire a shot from a pistol.

At a certain point the sound cannot be heard.

There you'll have found the acoustic node,
and to the eye it is invisible.

Let three persons group themselves
at certain points
around a completely placid lake surface
and shout alternately to one another "here"—
in a certain rhythm.

In no time at all the shout "here" will come
uninterrupted from all directions
and nobody will be able to distinguish
his voice from the others.

What a delicate antiphon!

And a little electric bell,
place it under a jar hermetically sealed
after the air has been pumped out,
soon it becomes inaudible,
just as you might have expected.

Thus all suspicions are confirmed
regarding the imperfection of the medium of conveyance,
its peculiar talent for acting on its own.

On its own, on its own.

The time that's left is always very short.
Sounds are only produced by the solitary person.
The winter is very cold. All the boats are ice bound.

And in clear weather, skates, the red sleighs
that sound like little bells
under the "sealed jar."

Silence, somebody speaks, is it you, is it me?

Echo, delicate nymph, with your muted voice.

[C.M.]

The Bridges of Königsberg

In the Prussian city of Königsberg
there's an island called the Kneiphoff;
two branches of the river Pregel flow around it,
seven bridges cross the two branches.

Seven bridges. Never more than one at a time.
Now almost everywhere water can be heard.
It is blind water, black water,
nocturnal water. Three varieties of water.

Churches and towers and green sloping roofs.
Here is a staircase. Here is a house.
Here is the dog barking in the garden.
It is black, quite black. It is barking.

Years. Years and days. Alike as . . .
Can't you hear me? I'm shut inside,
and nobody is listening. As Euler's hemispheres
in Magdeburg. As unalike as apples.

An ordinary October, fresh, the dogs barking,
voices, and only one bridge at a time;
never to walk across the same bridge twice.
Some children only step on every third cobblestone.

Only on every third. Lure of the Abyss.
The third door that always creaks.
Years. Years and days. *Can't you hear me?* October,
and still no frost in the air.

In order to walk across the seven bridges,
one after another and across each only once,
you need, so the mathematician Euler says,
actually an eighth. There is no eighth bridge.
Goddamn ice that will not freeze.

[C.M.]

A Story from Russia

There are some kinds of bigger building
in which the windows don't quite match the house.
The result is a glare that is unendurable.
It's the windows do the glaring.

A thin gentleman visiting one of the chancelleries
forgets a roughknit glove. He walks away. The glove
is found by Y. It is bitterly cold. Y. puts it on,
and, being mistaken for Z., soon runs into trouble.

And we enter the primeval forests of European culture.
Tragedies, identities mistaken, rakish parties—
when all is said and done, what curious patterns give
a shape to fate. Monsieur A., all alone
"parmi les proses écrasées de sa jeunesse."

But, outside the texts, an absolute stillness, winter night.
Scrutinize history and it might as well not have occurred.
History: princes, rebellions, stories. A darkness.
Bitter cold, clearest moonlight, not even the track of a sleigh.

It's the windows do the glaring.

[C.M.]

The Living and the Dead

Ice-ferns on the window.
Crystals that will grow in caustic soda,

"blind" and in discernible forms.
Strindberg saw a sketch for living

and the longing of dead things
to come to life.

The stuffed animal that a child has carried everywhere
and warmed in bed until the toy gets a name

and all the family talks about it
as they would talk about a well-known person.

Tin soldiers with their sad, immobile faces.
The Moorish trumpeter that sits on high

above the splendid organ works in Oliva
and at a predetermined moment lifts the trumpet

and blows in three directions. He is a Moor.
All things imitating life will fail

and do not fool us.

Yet about these things, crystals
toys, trumpeter,

remains an air of sorrow, of wistfulness.
And *this* is not an imitation.

We recognize it at once.
And are reminded of ourselves.

[H.W.]

Elegy

The small tin boxes holding screws. The small
boxes with their trademarks half rubbed off,

originally meant for something else,
now contain screws. Nothing but screws.

Late-autumn day, the strong wind brings crows,
a dozen, whirling and flapping at the roadside.

Plato, grown old like a teacher of small boys,
in a grubby sweater, regards them without passion,

knowing that their archaic idiom is
Ionian dialect. Impenetrable.

In rainy weather the Forms do not exist.

Once I too had a form to see with
and so could understand the world I saw.

One of these small tin boxes carries an emblem,
a gold medal: *First Prize, Amsterdam.*

Now it contains screws. Nothing but screws.

What other birds do I know?
The wren. Field-lurker, songless.

The wren at dusk between the hills and the houses.
Resting a moment at the side of the ditch.

Perfectly still in flying.

[P.M.]

Three Poems from the New World

I   "The Perfectionists" Colony in Oneida N.Y.

Countless shadows populate this world,
men's, women's, infants' voices
small as the crickets under the trees.

In large deserted white rooms in a gigantic house
there came a surprising acid scent,
as of a white, foreign bread or timber,

the white church beat its noon
and at 10,000 meters high, soundlessly,
and visible only as a hazy line,

the plane from Montreal to Boston.
The year 1848: bank crashes and pamphlets,
disused furnaces and a house under high elms:

"here for thirty years lived hundreds of men and women
in total sexual and economic community:
they ran a glassworks and a new order of things."

In some places there are still signs of the glassworks,
a kind of specially thick, opaque fragments.
Of the dream a sour scrubbed smell lingers.

John Humpert Noyes, Jefferson and Thoreau,
all dreamers with steely-gray sharp eyes.
Their images pursue me in the dream,

I dream that their guilt or innocence
is my innocence or share of the world.
There is no way that leads out of history.

And Mr. T. in his white house with high pillars tells
of the woods at Adirondack in 1790 and the American brook trout:
"a lively little fellow who is found only in very clear water."

II *Maple Syrup*

For the small children in the New World who fretted and cried
their mothers would cook a syrup of maple sap.

This taste remains: an acid, clear-yellow liquid,
burnt sugar, fresh sap and something else, unknown:

I convince myself that this is the taste of America: maple syrup.
Concord and Los Alamos, Utica and the killings in Mississippi.

And the boy hunting squirrels with his gun beneath the trees.
This enigma is too hard for me: I thought there was innocence,

but never that it could be as thick as prison walls.
I have never felt this acid taste before, this sap,

but I knew it must exist: here it is everywhere,
in the tepid air, it blends into the strong neon lights.

and it is inside the unreal white choirs of the churches.
Fredrika Bremer saw this world and called for justice,

a justice would include the oppressors also.
I understand her now. Whoever has felt this remarkable taste,

its acid, will never again take the word "innocence" in his mouth
without feeling how it grows on his tongue, how it slowly
    changes . . .

III The Wright Brothers Look for Kitty Hawk
In an agitated dream I saw everything explained:

Otto Lilienthal soars impressively in his glider
down the steep hill in Grosslichterfelde.

A fierce wind was blowing, fine for kites,
and someone monotonously talked about "the gnostic darkness."

It was a warning, a whisper that came and went.

Bakunin steps aboard the cargo-steamer *Andrew Steer,*
one spring day, in the harbor of Nikolaevsk, among sheds and out-
houses.

In the 19th century the sea often smells musty in a calm.
The revolutions are being prepared. Seafire sparkles.

And Milton Wright, bishop in The Church of the United Brethren,
presents his sons Wilbur and Orville with one of Pénaud's models:

not unlike a misformed bird with a hungry neck.
Wind-tunnel experiments at the cycle factory's range

and the dry sand smoking in stubborn wind.
What is bad or good about a kite? It flutters,

rises in a sudden rush but with a dead motion
at the moment when it should tear the thread,

the much too short thread. In Africa the locomotives rust,
and the steamship *Savannah* with fluttering streamers

over the unreal blue sea. Solemn smoke.
Nature is always tangible: the straddle-helm and the propeller.

Dresden. Hanoi. And "the gnostic darkness."

[R.F.]

Concert for Mechanical Blowers

(after Grandville)

You must imagine a storm, a real storm.
Only in a storm do the words scatter sufficiently.
And then sentences form.

The blowers, thirty in number,
in exact rows, fixed on mechanical pivots
with meaningless trumpets of brass,

the same expressions as on figures
small figures you see in toyshops.
What does the expression on figures in toyshops mean?

It's sledging weather. Restless steam is hissing. Who's in control?
Who are we waiting for? We're waiting for the Mechanical Boy
who with a metallic boy's voice rattles off syllables.

Storm, a real storm, the clouds chase each other.
Turnips and motherly pumpkins take their place,
carrots take their place and an old-fashioned well pump.

Isn't there a human being then? No.
There isn't a person here, *not a single person!*
The hare swims in the sea and the fish in the rye

for it's a storm, you see, a real storm,
it's something else! It's a storm.
Now they swivel on their pivots once in each direction.

Then the sheets of paper blow out of the chemist's files
and scatter to the winds like mad snow.
High up in the Alps where they are found

they are charred. White against black. The hare in the sea.
The fish in the rye. Thirty trumpeters, each on his pivot

Death, stay thy phantoms.

[R.F]

On the Deepest Sounds

There is a pipe in big organs,
the thirty-two-foot basso, the contrabassoon,

huge vibrating pillar of air, late autumn
when water rises in the wells,

the subterranean network of waters and wells,
and it is more a sorrow than a sound.

At this lower limit where the music ends,
something different wants to begin.

Body more than sound, body and darkness,
and late autumn, when the wells are rising,

but since it is lower than earth,
lower than music, lower than lament

—it does not want to begin, it does not begin,
and therefore it does not exist.

Now it is closer, now it is distinct!
Now it will soon be audible, far and wide.

[C.M.]

Notes on the 1860s

George Boole's book on the laws of thought appeared in 1844;
that's three years before Baudelaire's *Les Fleurs du Mal.*

In Boole's book the seed of the computer is to be found,
the ticking relays, the vacuum tubes of the future.

With charming innocence this algebra teaches us
that every set has something in common with the "empty set."

The empty set. In a dream I meet Baudelaire,
small, transparent, dark shadows under his eyes,

and I insist that he comment on Boole.
He accepts this request as being altogether natural

and starts with a quotation from the Marquis de Sade:

"Nothing floods us with fear and lust so much
as knowledge of the ticking relays, the vacuum tubes,

murmurs that come from the hotter mineshafts of the future."

All of a sudden he checks himself, as if he'd said too much.

"Sir, we walk on ice polished by the wind. You understand?

We live in a time when the wind is rising."

[C.M.]

from Declaration of Love to a Sephardic Lady

(Events in 1939)

. . . . at last broad daylight
over the vast landscape, the frozen lakes,
down through the clear ice more and more blue
down to the ice-bound burbot who look

with their great wide open eyes and see everything
without being startled, down through the secrets,
and over the great stretches of water white ice-light,
the stones of the islands rise up like reproaches

small boys on their way across the ice, small boys
in red caps pulling their sledges across the ice,
they've pulled them all day since early dawn
and the solemn gurgling sound under the ice,

it's midday, March 1969, Europe's intellectuals
still remain, the ancient bank palaces remain,
the small visiting cards in staircases remain,
and all feel a secret anxiety, but out here on the ice

there are only small boys, small boys in red caps
pulling their sledges stubbornly northwards. Between islands
in the south, there are cracks of open water, it is time,
it is high time, it is time says the stubborn wind

time, wind and broad daylight, crack-formation, thaw,
it is time say the agitated birds across there
moving over the ice like a flock of irresolute punctuation marks
that won't stop for long on any paper

it is time, it is always time say the burbot eyes,
there's still time says the clock, little time
say the agricultural specialists, it is time
says someone and rises in a glade in the forest,

it is time say I and I don't know for what,
and daylight, but never again with the same color,
a gentle golden ecstatic color,
like the gold background of Byzantine pictures

which was still there when I was four years old.

Of the last years of the thirties
I spent the greater part on a kitchen floor
over whose blue and white squares the light fell
from a window facing westwards.

In summer the blind
was drawn half down, completely yellow,
and this golden light washed across the floor.
Was this how it began?

19 Floragatan, now to be demolished,
inhabited by a "grandmother" so called
without really being one;
in her living room with stoves

there was the same light behind very tall curtains,
and memories from a spell in Asia.
"Times of India. Supplement" 1903-1907,
with pictures of floods, railway-inaugurations,

the Raj of Naipur and the wedding of the viceroy's daughter,
and in a sandalwood cabinet small strange gods
who ruled the world with eight arms,
this very lean dry "grandmother"

wore her hair up, back over the ears
in a way which thirty years later
in quite another part of the story
should prove I must have loved her.

She died in the warm summer of 1939
and the yellow light held sway in the room alone.

It is time say I and don't know for what:
some secretive memory of a gold-yellow light
returns like a streak out of the past
(the past's wardrobe door with a little slit)

one of the first days of April 1969
like a signal from a sinking steamer
or like a signal from someone very remote
who is trying to reach me and doesn't know any other language

and so the child signals to the adult,
myself to myself with incomprehensible warnings
from another decade when the world was yellow
a decade more or less spent on a kitchen floor.

So they go, I would say, the sounds in the world,
they go out and come back to one another.

My five year old son, still in some freedom
which lets him feel everything around him,
every thought, knows at once what I want
and hands me a sketch of a "death's head."

It's the same picture he and other small fellows
draw with chalk on all the hoardings of the district,
skull, crossbones, gaping mouth,
the same I drew at the same age,

the same we all draw at that age,
before the hairy triangles, the sex words,
up on the hoardings as if they wanted to reveal
some mighty secret. "Death's head," crossbones,

is that also a secret desire? And the children know;
but only at a special age. In Jerusalem,
the Arab quarters, I saw the children play hopscotch
and the pattern had the same shape as on Frankegatan in 1939:

two hemispheres, divided by a square,
the same shape as the Etruscan soothsayers' *templum*,
the upper world. Ours, which is square.
And below it an underworld the same shape as the sky.

Playing hopscotch is a divination rite.

Where do the children's rites, games, cults come from,
these self-evident peculiarities with strings,
stones, marbles, burning-glasses, wall-words,
this language which takes possession of them?

Who began it? Who leads them into the rite?

In the beginning of April almost everyone dies:
I mean everyone who has long wished to die,
the old white-haired women with thigh-fracture
who all winter haven't had a visit from anyone,

the pale restless alcoholics with thin hands;
you can meet them in the hospital corridor
where they are rolled out on their stretchers,
and with an ash-gray color as if they belonged

to some other genus and give an impression
of being *physically larger* than ourselves
but powerless, just as there is a moment
two or three minutes before the umbilical cord is cut

when the newborn with his thunder-blue complexion
seems to belong to another genus
and appears foreign and *physically large.*
Later we regard him as a human and forget.

In the same way at the beginning of April each year
I also have a feeling of dying
or that this is the proper time to die,
and if I don't want to I must begin to live.

False spring sun, secret hope,
each year and the same soft spring rain on the fields.
Gone the soft snow that sheltered and warmed
the oblivion replaced by roving memories,

the red sledges vanish out of sight,
the small boys on the ice are seen no more;
and suddenly another season. Suddenly time to live,
or to decide, since others die,

on some name to call this that I'm living.

How does one live? One produces one's own life
said one of those learned gentlemen from 1860
who still stare at us from the portraits.
North Europe, April 1969. An "active life," or how?

"By accident," "by compromises"?
By chance, or "beneath cast-iron vaults"?

Many spectacles, and frowns,

for spring freshly aired clothes, involved grammar,
and sometimes a feeling that my voice vanishes
as the voices vanished in those railway cathedrals
from last century where white steam billows against the roof,

(the same white steam billows in a picture by Piranesi
long before the age of mechanics and without the railway
it becomes impressive and frightening)

In this kind of noise every word gets lost.

Robinson on the island, already on the first day begins
to change: originally a dull and indifferent youngster,
and during the journey still only half captivated
by everything new he sees, and the water's roaring,
wakes up clear-eyed and fashions clever tools

everything is still to be done and the shore is endless possibility,
with its stones, pieces of driftwood, mussels,
"the world's great age begins anew."
Clear-eyed he goes away from us into the greenery
and this is not the beginning but the end

of a long and melancholy youth.
When Robinson has reached his island, shipwrecked
and thus sees that he is alone
he has his greatest loneliness behind him.

Where is the island that changes our lives
and forces us to begin again at the beginning,
fashion tools, plough fields, fire clay
out of the vague memories we carry with us?

Where is the island that changes our lives?

It happens against a gold background,
the almost forgotten gold background of a childhood,
and that background is, in what follows,
just background, the foreground is more difficult:

and all the time I go astray against that background,
so the picture which should appear
never emerges properly, for the sake of mere background:
thus I still remember a gold-yellow light from the fifties,

I lived very high, five floors up,
and the window itself seemed to be
in the crown of a huge tree whose branches in summer
gave shade: a very lonely time, in that room,

with teapot and books, manuscripts and days,
and some kind friend who sometimes came in
(we talked about the events of the fifties)
we used to watch the tree's branches stirring

no not the branches but their shadows
against the wallpaper some such June evening,
and it was yellow, ecstatically yellow
in the same way, and I looked at them and thought:

the background of my life, a secret color,
and against it the picture will be drawn,
and I still have no picture and don't know,
and wrote at night some quiet poem

which treated of night, or of water,
of light and haze, or ice, my pet theme,
and some small fellows on their way across the ice
it was a time when almost everything was on the move

and I remember those eating-places
with the air thick with smoke, where we talked
of the world's concerns as if the world
was a storehouse for anecdotes,

and once, when I should have been catching a train,
how I came to be sitting on grass, emerald-green
(it was in the beginning of May 1958)
talking with a fine-limbed good-looking girl,

and how we talked without talking at all
and once more how that yellow light gleamed
and there came years of virtual emptiness, something
hung over me, difficult to say what,

but that yellow time I remember clearly.

That train must have gone very far.

It is time I thus say, and don't know,
and daylight and time and I know I deceive you
yes just deceive you with that yellow
which returns only against my will

and forces me to talk, about that yellow
which, strictly speaking irrelevant and remote,
the whole time prevents me talking, clearly,
about something else which I want to tell.

It exists in darkness. It lives in darkness.
With a weak gold gleam in the middle of the dark.
It is a favorable darkness. Like winter
when the soft snow . . . and the light of a lamp,

tracks of animals in the snow and burbot in the ice
and one who walks with the lamp through the snow,
happy about the surrounding tracks
which prove that though unseen they were there,

the hares, the big white hares, the roe-deer
with blood from their feet, the foxes,
and the frost can be heard, the greatest cold has a sound,
and later in the night a clock that stops

with the cold, where it hangs on an outside wall
and at last the faint red streak
of morning light, but very weak, and deep red,
and more tracks in the snow, and the lamp

and then the whole sky red, March 1969,
the medieval world remains at night,
but each night vanishes with dawn,
first blood-red, then gray-white

against the snow . . .

(An episode in Berlin)
One year later I wanted to tell
E., a wiser friend,
what actually happened.

It was in a park in Berlin, the autumn leaves were falling,
small snow flakes were falling, the statues froze,

it was already late autumn.

E. listened closely; there shone
intelligence and interest

in his small ancient reptile face.

(Some reptiles are friendly
and then show an indulgent affection

for our lesser wisdom.)

So I told him. We walked between marble sculptures.

That on the edge of a desert I came to know
a lady, woman, girl

who made me painfully conscious of my third year

(without my being able to grasp why)

how she moved with light
dancelike steps,
so slender she gave an impression
of being very tall
without being so,
the long black hair
(which had been very easy to pleat)
and which with a characteristic gesture
she brushed behind her small fine ears,
about her small girlish breasts,
the short sudden bursts of laughter,

her neck's slim line down to her back
and the very faint scent of myrrh,

her complete lack of musical sense,
her views on Botticelli

(there is something agonized in his paintings,
also "The Birth of Venus" is a catastrophe)

and how in a remarkable way, almost without words,
she changed me, more and more,
so that I no longer felt bitterness,

only sorrow,

no longer winter, clinking October ice
under the feet of schoolchildren where they walk

in the dawn

no longer snow, but sorrow, a sudden sorrow,

the mildest sorrow

E. listened intently.

He didn't answer.

And the snow fell thicker and thicker

over the frozen park

(*Symphonie Phantastique*)
over the vast landscape
weariness comes sneaking, gray like February
in Strindberg's Stockholm, Södra Bergen 1879,
gray like the polar convoys to Murmansk 1942

no I'm not talking about something private,
weariness is not something private, it is a language,
but in a private person it feels like something private,
when weariness comes sneaking it is coming to me,

"Sing Cuckoo sing, Death is a Comedy!"

The thinkers who knew the truth went astray
while trout fishing in the Adirondacks
and they mixed the lake's glass-clear water
with American Bourbon for a quenching drink

and when the students in Berlin in the tear-gas clouds
paused for a moment they found that
despite the gas they were breathing differently,
since 1965 we have been breathing differently;

not nervously but more calmly, see the truth
more straight in the eye, and lie first
when we try to speak, Central Park
on Sunday evenings you can see Hippies

dancing naked in the grass, a midsummer night's dream
and Prospero with his wand can't even conjure
the storm that rages somewhere in the stillness.

Skolimowski: "Polish Analytical Philosophy"

gives an account in footnotes of the fates, internments,
executions that struck the century's reasonable people.

Only the foolish are left and the grammar
can no longer lay the same claim on us

as still in 1963: "now we're going into a strange world,"

now the fools are dancing with their rattles,
the last European intellectuals
died in the Warsaw ghetto in 1942 and we
who still read their books barely know

that they are gone ("Polish Analytical Philosophy")
that we are alone and not even the grammar,
no not even it, and in a time of absurdity
we must have confidence in our folly,

that also folly will learn to shine
like some blue-white lamp, and it can,
but shining is not everything, besides
have we ever defined our thoughts?

They think in us and we listen, to the storm
whose inaudible roar grows, and the sail,
which begins to catch sounds from far away,
the murmur in Oneida Community's dining hall

with the news about Fort Sumter,
or in the Chaconne of Rameau's "Dardanus"
an assonance which no one had credited with a hidden meaning,
a metaphor theory in Chladenius which comes true,

and nothing can any longer redeem the other
to order and relationship, nothing,
weariness comes sneaking, the kind
of sneaking weariness as before tropical thunder

schizophrenia becomes a way of life
and healthier than the helpless attempts
"to find a normal voice-pitch"
Sing Cuckoo sing, Death is a Comedy!

Pictures out of childhood's yellow rooms captivated me,
they fell like rain, rose like birds
out of a marsh in spring, rose and vanished,
their twittering so loveless, so empty!

The tiny pictures, the tiny strokes
of the tiny signs, the philosophers' alphabet
which won't ever do, the philosophers
who all the time seem to be talking of something else,

the playground's dreadful lavatory smell
blended with the scent of poplars, the feeling
of a whole childhood surrounded by enemies,
and the feeling of the need to compromise for peace,

the stinking lavatories, the lean assistant master
who fights, white in the face, with black gloves!
Appalling gray-white light; do we feel terror
more as children, or do we hide less?

The same stink was the first I felt in
1968 during a visit to Osviezcim,
the locos shunt in the mist, the child's terror,
it is always the same blue-white light, and terror

ice-white as in the polar sea, the ships' dark smoke,
I'm on my way to Murmansk with a polar convoy,
Murmansk 1942, of two hundred ships four
only four will reach harbor in Murmansk:

and the philosophers won't explain
why reality is so unreal,
won't explain: seven children walk in the jungle,
they're foreign, seven children

walk in line with their hands forward
resting forward on each other's shoulders,
are they imitating a train? If they
have never seen a train what are they imitating?

Weariness comes sneaking.
I see my life as compromises,
weary compromises, compromises
make it unreal: restless watchman

in the lunatic asylum's pale dayroom, surrounded
by schizophrenics. After about ten years
you can see some situations recur,
even see people recur

(naturally also cowardice recurs)
and the same people recur in new opinions
the same lack of considered opinion as before:
we must have confidence in madness instead,

and I have still not talked about myself,
madness is not something private, it is a language,
but in a private person it feels private
when madness comes sneaking

(since 1965 we've dreamt differently)
it comes to me also and blows
like the fable cat in a silver horn, walks
like the fable cat in seven league boots

and the cat walks and walks, in committees there is whispering,
and the smell, the stink of urine and death,
and poplars, the convoy goes towards Murmansk,
they're flying with nuclear weapons over Iceland,

in four less read collections a poet talks
about a deep, a gorge, "and one doesn't hear it"
and the pictures rise like birds, fall like snow,
in an underground nuclear weapon store in Kansas

there's a microscopic fault in some time-circuit,
the fine workings are activated, they tick,
"and one doesn't hear it," and the cat is walking
and there is terror and terror, and one

is not terror of dying but terror
that one lives, terror at our own coldness,
the smaller lies and the irresolution,
and that is why Harold Lloyd

in his foremost work, at last, in the fugue of vertigo,
"Facade climbing sequence," looks most frightened
a moment towards the end when he is hanging
inches above the pavement but doesn't dare

doesn't dare look down, and the cat is walking
in its boots, and only once
did I seem to see how across my gold background
a head appeared, how someone saw me

"over the deeps" with dark eyes
and it was You, strange beauty,
and it became very still, the green
stones in Your belt shone strangely

and my madness took a secret meaning
from Your beauty which like a sharp pain
penetrated a decade of weariness
and read the weariness like a cipher,

and the cat is walking, and it became still:
A Sephardic lady with stones in her belt,
it is You, You look at me through the storm
and in the middle of the fugue of vertigo everything stops

and the large hand on the clock rescues me,
I hang onto the hand of a clock that's ticking,
we know that death can be mass-produced
and everyone's way of talking, *everyone's,* to me,

since I was twelve, shows that they have lied,
all have the pitying expression with which
you want to conceal that someone is already deceived,
all but You, and the cat is walking in its boots

over the seas, over the dateline, time zones,
demarcation lines, minefields, watchtowers,
the cat is walking with its soft steps in the night,
soon daybreak . . .

(*The story of the great drawing shaft at Blankstöten*)
The great Polhem built the drawing winch at Blankstöten.
He believed that mechanics was an alphabet,
the new era's script which would fill the world
and draw through a vast landscape

its *Kunstgezeuge,* push-rods, gear-complexes,
creaking wood, screeching iron, timberwork,
in forward and backward movements which blindly
led forces from one place to the other.

Of all these ingenuities the drawing shaft,
where a mighty wheelhouse was adorned with four streamers,
was the greatest of all: from a two hundred foot depth
barrels were raised on hooks towards the light,

and the power was altered through cogwheels as high as the church
        tower.
It was a new kind of world and through the summer night
it was heard like a roar of great forces: it was Man

who for a few short days ruled the world. The foetus
in its microcosmos hears the song of the remote galaxies,
how the radio noise comes and goes, like the blood's murmuring,
and when a giant star implodes with its own weight,

and falls *inwards* and turns its own light to darkness
the foetus knows. And birds know their own direction,
and some very icy night with a clear starry sky
you can hear, if you are soon to die, the giant roar

of remote galaxies slowly swinging round on their midpoint.

In May some birchwood stands very light,
Christopher Polhem, in the blue dress coat, walks
and listens to the cuckoo's song. It's a day in May.
It's the day when the wind turns. The leaves rustle.

Of the drawing shaft there remains a log-pile,
peculiar clearings in a boggy wood,
and a few gigantic iron fittings corroding with rust.

The streamers fluttered in the wind, the water rustled,
the gigantic wheel only just bore its own weight,
and there was more ingenuity than wood and iron can bear.

In the depths of Your dark eyes, far in, I have seen
how something shone with a gleam that outdoes gold's.
Under Your heavy eyelid that secret is preserved,

unknown beautiful with slim very cool hands
you know it already and you still say nothing:
The great wheel broke under its own weight,

and this *kunstgezeuge* in all its ingenuity, its beauty,
was driven by water, till it broke, for four days.

And You who never walked among the birches still know:
The great drawing shaft was a dream.

The great Polhem built the drawing shaft of Blankstöten.

(*"Pain is a fire. Powerfully she changes into
smoke our heart's beloved idols and in the flames'
bath she purifies our souls."* Stagnelius, Elegy)
"Pain is a fire."
And the wave of violence
powerfully rising.
Those mutilated.
Those hung in the trees.

Those thrown in the wells.
The dead children in the school bus
blasted by a mine.
On clear days the condensation streaks of the planes
when they are returning towards afternoon.
"And powerfully she changes."

I went through strange underground rooms
and could no longer see.
So it is to be blind.
I was not afraid, wanted only to know
the place's measurements, its geometry,
depth, height, the sea horizon.
It was a labyrinthine prison,
an imagined prison
but imagined not by me but by someone else.
So it is to be blind.

In reality I have been blind for a long time
but never came to think of it.
It is hard to be blind
since all the time one must say goodbye.
"Goodbye" one says
as if the word were easy.
But goodbye is hard.
I know, for, believe me,
nearly everything I've done means goodbye.
If only I were on the wrong planet I'd leave it.
But I'm not on a planet.
I'm in a labyrinth, the wrong labyrinth.

I walked in some blind rooms,
or walked, myself blind, in some rooms.
Then someone came and walked beside me.
For long she walked in silence.

I pretended not to notice her
but heard her light steps
and knew she wore thin sandals.
I heard her breathing,
the faint sound of her dress
touching her knees.
I reached my hand out. She took it.

You are my Anima, I said.
First, two or three years old,
I confused you with a grandmother Emma
who lived in some yellow rooms
where the curtain stirred in the wind.
Then I didn't see you again for many years.

Next time I saw you, you were a Sephardic lady
who smiled at me in a café in the desert
and I recognized you at once. You are beautiful.

But you are no grandmother
and you are no Sephardic lady.
You are my Anima, and I don't know you.

Don't leave me, you must tell me what you see!

For long she walked in silence
and I had almost given up hope
when she answered with a question:

Where are you going?

And I answered:
Where you're going.
Towards peace. Another kind of peace.
Lead me where you wish,
if only you lead me to peace.

And walking in this way

with our fingers twined together
we went further and further into the night

Of each other we knew little.

(If I forget your face
I promise to remember your voice
and I'll remember it as a voice in darkness

immediately before dawn, at last broad daylight
. . . .)
[R.F.]

Warm Rooms and Cold

We go from warm rooms to cold
and from cold to warm again.

Someone being born cries suddenly at the light.
He knew all along the landslide was coming.

How many mysterious cities underground
are built by what we call the heart!

Intercourse is a way of remembering rather than forgetting.

Sometimes we're dry snow crystals
driven by ice cold winds, whirling

over a large shiny ice surface. Without mercy.

Large warm summer days under immense trees
royal deer graze in the green shade.

A mild wind goes through the landscape.

I mean, our complaining must also come to an end.

                                              [Y.L.S.]

Song of Equilibrium

I often say to myself,
I'm in equilibrium, it all balances

I walk around with a little song on my lips

only tightrope, which becomes slacker the longer I walk
but just a bit, only momentarily,

and it doesn't seem like the wind
this wind that's blown up,

would increase and strengthen,
and if it did, who knows,

maybe it isn't so hard to walk a tightrope
in a storm either, comparatively few people have tried it,

when all's said and done,

and where else would I walk?

We often say to ourselves,
It's in equilibrium, it all balances

the topmost blocks of stone are balancing
on the lower blocks, and the lower blocks

on some still lower, and they in their turn—

well! What a remarkable edifice,
what a mighty line, what a challenge,

and just imagine, it's standing, you wouldn't believe it
unless you knew it was all in equilibrium,

it all balances, what would happen otherwise?

I often say to myself, I'm in equilibrium, it all balances.

I sleep at night and wake up in the morning,

everything functions quite well,

I answer the right number when the phone rings,

and some people who call have always dialed wrong,
they don't want me, they want someone else.

I always answer with the right name
when they call me, with the right name,

and when death points at someone, he always
points at someone else who goes at once,

where else would he go?

We often say to ourselves,
we're in equilibrium, it all balances,

the rains arrive on time

and the wars come to those other places
and the rat on the rope and the rope on the butcher

currencies stay at the right rate,

what matters is having the right feeling,
the right point of view, the right composure,

the right—well!

And the boy leaves for school on the dot.

[Y.L.S.]

The Discords

Faint smell of citronella from summers
before 1939, something about a green frog

and already in that grass the knowledge
of having a strange life before you.

A very old woman I know
had a strange congenital malformation:

from in front it looked like two noses
or one nose cloven in two.

In the Old People's Home she moved
with the same natural dignity

you otherwise find only in outstanding beauties:

she knew she was carrying something tremendous through the world

and she was quite right.

Anyone she met and looked at
with her kind, watery blue eyes

had to put his own life in question,
had to take recourse in the secret life of God.

In Stravinsky's Concerto in D-major, in the middle
there's a wonderful discord

an old Russian chorale that's lost its way in red glass

and shattered into a thousand fragments in the glass—

at the outer limits there's a tremendous
terrible freedom, no one stops us

except ourselves

AND EVERYTHING AT ONCE.

[Y.L.S.]

Darkness

About my other side
the side that's turned away
my uninhibited side:

Darkness in darkness
and furthest into the darkness
something to wrestle with

strong enough to whirl me off like a leaf.

[Y.L.S.]

Poem on Revisionism

Puzzled fly
shut in a night express

still trying to fly
and doing remarkably well

From the south end of the train it arrives at the north
already a far wiser fly

and the train roars all the faster into the night

[P.M.]

Lines for the Prince of Venosa*

We leave Robinson here

he was nothing but a character in an adventure story
that everyone's read before.

In November 1971 it was windy (as usual)
a terrible storm, the planes couldn't land.

I sat up until late
with some people in Gothenburg

and understood they didn't understand me (as usual),
fetching up in Lund the next afternoon—

I almost said Holy Lund,
for the wind suddenly stopped blowing.

Professor Ehrenswärd was sitting
behind a very small desk.

During our conversation he kept sucking a milk carton
as if it were a mother's nipple

and he told me about the world of the future,
about the sailing ships, the hordes of cyclists

going out to the fields at dawn,
the charcoal kilns, the little inns

* Gesualdo, Italian composer (c. 1560-1613), who had his first wife,
Maria d'Avalos, murdered with her lover (Ed.).

along the rained-out roads, the sects,
the trains of flagellants, seafarers on a long voyage

to America, the madrigal singing and the reed flutes
in the wide sweep of gardens in April,

proletarians of the plow tilling the soil,
and high up, floating slowly

on the moonlit side of the clouds, the voyagers
in their hot-air balloons.

Yes

beauty is the only thing that lasts.

And I thought of the stones, the stones pure and simple,

because they live so slowly

that they don't even discover our existence.

(Certain quartzes, Caillois tells us,
contain some trapped water
older than all the seas in our world
and it swishes around in the stone's darkness
like a very small, very clean sea.)

Yes

beauty is the only thing that lasts.

It doesn't matter a damn how you misuse your life
you'll still find a way home to yourself

although naturally it isn't the home
you left, faraway.

Mahler and Bruckner wrote enormous slow symphonies
to convince us that death isn't so bad after all;

like the Swedes in the nineteen-seventies
they lived in a technologically advanced monarchy

which no longer believed in itself,
where the postal system already functioned irregularly.

Mahler and Bruckner is a congenial firm;
the immensely slow adagio which closes

Mahler's Ninth Symphony ought to get an award
just like penicillin or polio vaccine.

Together with Mahler and Bruckner,
both of them wearing soulful little eyeglass frames,

stubbornly swaddled in the lap robes against the evening chill,
I went by jeep to an unusually nice place,

the monastery of St. Catherine in the Sinai desert,
an unreal place between red mountains

with admittedly minor parking problems.

Together we viewed the Codex Sinaicus,
the first handwritten manuscript in a Slavic tongue,

demonstrating that Bishop Cyrillus of Ohrid
wasn't so stupid after all

the way those Byzantine louts had always claimed.

And then the guide insisted on showing us the ossuary.
Mahler with Guide Bleu and Bruckner with a cigar

were amazed that the bones of bishops were always kept together
while all other bones are sorted according to kind

as in wholesales Whitman,

"Wrists, and wrist-joints, hand, palm, knuckles, thumb, forefinger,
   finger-joints, finger-nails"

neatly as in a spare parts warehouse
every damn finger-joint there was in St. Catherine's

nicely sorted and logged by those Bedouins
who were slaves in the monastery during the early Middle Ages.

It's just like at home in the Cathedral of St. Stephen,
Mahler said, as we came out, putting on his sunglasses,

(the light in the Sinai is nothing to fool with)

(a kind of intense primaeval light over naked mountains
and a man riding becomes immense,
in his dark cloak, a single man
can fill a square mile with solemn presence).

It's because the bishops have to *pull themselves together*
first on the Last Day, Bruckner said,

they must *get on their legs* quickly to take command,
Mahler suggested, like some kind of reserve lieutenants,

"I beat and pound for the dead," said Mahler,
"I blow through my embouchures my loudest and gayest for them."

Yes.

The wind stopped blowing over Holy Lund
and the guardrails on the turnpike were down for long stretches

as if a bad child had been playing with them.
An express train took me to Karlstad

where an old Lapp woman and a hearty football player
were going to read from their memoirs and I from mine.

(When the last decade was still young
Jack Kerouac went first class across the Atlantic.
In the dining room, the second day, he met
a little psychiatrist in gold-frame glasses and silver tie
who wanted to unravel his neuroses.
"Neuroses," Kerouac said, "inhibitions!"
"OK, now we'll see who's inhibited, you or me,
I'll count to three and then we'll drop our pants.")

The acoustics reminded me of the Sture Bath
and the next day the press opined that people from Värmland
generally are better writers
and that Gustafsson, above all, is unnecessarily *learned*

and in the midst of the confusion I saw, in the second row,

the beautiful young Donna Maria d'Avalos
with her red-gold hair, her wonderful lips,
her hairnet worked with pearls, oh ye gods!

Afterward I found her in the bar of the City Hotel
talking to a communist professor
and squabbling with a liberal councilman
at the next table. This gave me my chance.

Donna Maria, I said,
and she presented me with her prettiest smile.

And your husband, the Prince . . .

(I bit my tongue because I remembered a thing or two.)

The Prince, oh yes, the Prince, she answered impassively,

Yes he writes the most beautiful masses and madrigals . . .

Yes

beauty is the only thing that lasts

Mahler and Bruckner. Delicatessen.

A very small sea, completely dark,
trapped in age-old quartz.
Water that's never been in touch with water.
Wet before any dew had fallen
over the sterile desert mountains of our planet.

I came home one night around nine.
New snow had fallen. Already by the fence

my dog nipped my trouser cuffs, jumping about
in the snow. It's nice to feel loved.

[Y.L.S.]

San Francisco Sailing on Under the Earth

When the light falls across the hills
they light up like fire, one last moment,

the whole city drinks the light.

The first white men to see Alcatraz
found the island teeming with penguins:

solemn, comical birds who died easily.

The Chinese were called in by Morgan, ten dollars,
not in wages but once and for all

and died like flies building their railroads—
no Chinese women permitted

but ten or twelve came anyway,
all of Chinatown from eleven Chinese wombs

and the sick young girls from Canton
were locked up in cellars to die.

Emperor Norton, Sovereign Ruler of the United States
Protector of Mexico, Instigator of the Union Square Christmas tree

verdigris running along his epaulets

died easily one winter's night.

If you keep quiet you can hear the Creoles dancing.

Schooners, galleons, four-masters, barks
whole city districts consist of sunken ships

filled with sand, anchored like sisters
close to one another.

All of the Embarcadero rests on a subterranean fleet.

The Pan Am Building, the Bank of America
the skyscrapers are standing on decks far down in the depths

and that fleet sails on under the earth.

[Y.L.S.]

Brief Treatise on Seeing and Being Seen

Together with a half-blind sleeping dog
in a boat slowly drifting over the shoals at Enträ

and some late summer waves under a warm gray sky
rattling the gravel as they break over the shoals at Enträ.

And so I'm alone with the screeching gulls
who're no concern of mine, and with the memories,

the hopes, the voices, the faces of people
I've seen once and who've seen me

or the faces of those who've frightened me
who may have seen something special to frighten them.

And the feeling that somewhere I'm burning
like a salamander in the fire, somewhere I'm freezing

like a burbot in the ice, and they're both me.
And they won't merge, those pictures,

because pictures never want to merge,
so perhaps it's better without pictures;

and I remember the faces of German students
emerging from tear gas clouds, Berlin, 1968,

wearing expressions I didn't quite understand,
there was something they'd forgotten to tell me;

and from the prison at Ramleh I remember the Arab prisoners
walking round and round inside the barbed wire, three by three

looking at me ironically with wise brown eyes,
at me not at the guards or at the officers behind me,

only at me, and it was a moment of truth,
but I don't know what kind of truth;

and the gulls cry indifferently, hungrily,
drawing on the blackboard autumn has put up,

and it might be just before it rains or thunders,
or just before nothing in particular,

and when J., whom I hadn't seen for a long time,

said to me, It's impossible to love you,
it's impossible to love anyone, impossible,

there was a moment when she looked at me
with large questioning eyes, wanting to be contradicted;

and the waves rattling uncertainly over the shoals at Enträ,
the gulls are quiet again and it's only the dog

sleeping, half-blind like me, whimpering in his sleep.
He's deep in his dream, his warm furry

animal dream, I won't be able to follow him
into his dream and there's nothing but water

and waves rattling uncertainly over the shoals,
and, you understand, this poem might

continue indefinitely, and the same stones,
the same wise round stones that get older than we do,

would be rattled by the same wave in the same wind,
and I'm an eye just an eye seeing.

Shutting an eye can be just as difficult
as shutting an ear, believe it or not.

When a cloud comes between the sun and the northwest rose
        window
of Chartres Cathedral, the famous northwest rose window,

silent storms of color surge through the glass.

                              [Y.L.S.]

Sonnet I

The Desert by Rio Grande

Out of nothingness. *Ex nihilo.*
A song starts slowly. Music from the stone.
From stone contracted by the evening. Tone
sung by the siren stone. *Ex nihilo.*

River, tent, and branch, white bones dispersed
from cattle carcass here all things possess
shadows condensed into a nothingness.
The sharp-edged shadows are the things reversed.

As sharp as if a caged lark flew some place
under the ground. Here things and shadows fall
together, meet, and are compressed. The slow

song of stone: this day of light and space
which makes each day before it seem too small.
A song starts slowly. Tone *ex nihilo.*

[Y.L.S.]

Sonnet XVI

"The self, that king who rules over them":
wise Ekelöf means
that this might be the prince who unifies
a world of gliding shadows without home.

That world glimmers one foot under language;
full fathom five a father lies,
blind pearl his eyes washed by a deep-sea current.
With no word spoken he reigns over them.

So we are all princes! Stiff, medieval
shapes with a rod of iron in our hand,
we sit gravely at some well by night.

Its black surface trembles, the whole night
waits for this trembling. The realm lies
ravaged by frost. The ice on the well is thin.

[P.M.]

Sonnet XVII

Autumn storm, warm wind. Trees hide the moon.
Glimpse of the feeble-minded boy at table,
scraping the last out of his bowl. This earth,
this warm wind. Now from a darkening lake

a raw smell comes, as from a drowned body
floating unrecovered. And, made for life,
I walk through grass, hunting a word: one word
to express the damp autumnal smell, the moon

which watches anxiously over it all, the night
which only deepens, the window's yellow square
lighting a patch of garden, the damp earth

that smells of rotting pears, the cat that lurks
cunningly in the bushes. There was no rain.
I needed such a word.

[P.M.]

Sonnet XXIII

Your eyes. I knew it. I had kept nothing more:
your eyes only. Every other feature
was memory, and memory had stopped
at the minute of parting like a watch, and more

it could not tell. Hounds baying, more and more
faintly as the pack drew off. Another
landscape, as in Brueghel: jumbled together,
the sounds of crows, dogs, axes. Snow. And still more

snow, which covers everything. At twilight
the ponds freeze. After a year I saw you.
You came towards me, truth and memory

first wavered, then rushed stumbling forward: surely
the light from snow is the most *silent* light?
Same sorrow in the eye, same memory.

[P.M.]

Sonnet XXVIII

It comes late. It had some way to travel.
Although it has no name we call it sorrow.
A clenched fist is a fragile basket
of brittle finger-bones. To understand

your weakness is no easy matter. Few
can see their weakness as a mighty fortress.
You stand, let's say, in Gustav Adolf's Square
and know that you're deserted. To transcend

a place like that: hard, too. An open hand
is nearly always empty. And a cage
which never held a bird can easily give

a feeling of disorder. By what right
do we despise a liberty whose nature
consists in gently loosing every bond?

[P.M.]

Sestina on a Successful Volley

There was a time when every hour was whole
like the tennis ball that hangs for some
hundredth of a second, poised and waiting
above the net. Not "just" gone by, not "soon"
but some third thing, which is all we see.
The other is a hope for or a time

that's past, but not my own: another's time.
The dry thunk once again will make you whole.
Such are the only real things we see.
Hope and remembrance fill what seems to some
a largely random consciousness; we soon
see him standing, the next ball awaiting.

But who's the one standing beside him, waiting?
All time is eaten up by thoughts of time
that's past, or something that will happen soon.
Hope, and remembrance for the rest. The whole
man is the one no longer seeing some
other ball in that which he can see.

Those events we actually see
unexpectedly prove featureless. Waiting,
past years and late princes seem like some
frozen forms that live in frozen time.
With names we make the broken vessel whole,
carried with care to a well which soon

seems deep and full of mighty voices. Soon
a lonesome echo's left: and you can see
the surface of the water, light and whole.
Far down deep it lies so still and waiting.
It can't be reached. And it is you. Your time
is brief. A single stone suffices. And some

single surface breaks: transformed into some
thousand fragments whose reflections soon
flicker on the stone: and they are time.
The only time we understand. We see
in fragments. In frozen poses we stand waiting.
The dry thunk once again will make you whole.

We're living in some nameless world. We see.
We die as soon as we remember: waiting.
There was a time when every hour was whole.

[Y.L.S.]

Sestina

(from Sonnets, XXII)

You may begin at any point you choose.
In any case, we'll soon be back right here.
A silver-colored light is passing through
the marshy meadows, making them a home
for every tired thought. Did I see those
in childhood? From dream to dream. And often grief

for which there was no comfort. Not a grief
of common sort, but more a fact. I choose
to see it in this way: there is for those
who know too soon, *a limit* set: to here
you may proceed, no further. It is home,
but it is prison too. Time passes through

the grass in iambic meter, rippling through
the marshy grass, softly as if some grief,
borne on this wind, denied it growth. A home
is where dreams go, a place a dream will choose
above all others, sign that tracks lead here—
whether innocent or false. For those

tracks comprise the riddle. And with those
the road stops. The last picture coming through
grows from this marshy meadow. It knows. Here
but no further. Grass in the wind. My grief
is here and then at once: I do not choose.
The wind is moving every blade; my home

my self, all that is in me, lead me home
to voiceless places outside me; and those,
just as that telescope, my eye, may choose,
become inside out. A crack goes through
the wall, deceptive, false: it means some grief
that comes between us two, but only here

and not from here. Now I am coming here
to bring home my self, my grief; yes, home
to where my grief and everybody's grief
at last may coincide. I give back those:
Grass. And wind. You can see a landscape through
my face. Or vice versa, if you choose.

A road led here. A road for all of those
who see a home where summer winds pass through.
To freedom or to grief. Which do you choose?

[Y.L.S.]

Elegy for a Dead Labrador

Here there may be, in the midst of summer,
a few days when suddenly it's fall.
Thrushes sing on a sharper note.
The rocks stand determined out in the water.
They know something. They've always known it.
We know it too, and we don't like it.
On the way home, in the boat, on just such evenings
you would stand stock-still in the bow, collected,
scouting the scents coming across the water.
You read the evening, the faint streak of smoke
from a garden, a pancake frying
half a mile away, a badger
standing somewhere in the same twilight
sniffing the same way. Our friendship
was of course a compromise; we lived
together in two different worlds: mine,
mostly letters, a text passing through life,
yours, mostly smells. You had knowledge
I would have given much to have possessed:
the ability to let a feeling—eagerness, hate, or love—
run like a wave throughout your body
from nose to tip of tail, the inability
ever to accept the moon as fact.
At the full moon you always complained loudly against it.
You were a better Gnostic than I am. And consequently
you lived continually in paradise.
You had a habit of catching butterflies on the leap,
and munching them, which some people thought disgusting.
I always liked it. Why
couldn't I learn from you? And doors.
In front of closed doors you lay down and slept
sure that sooner or later the one would come
who'd open up the door. You were right.
I was wrong. Now I ask myself, now this
long mute friendship is forever finished,

if possibly there was anything I could do
which impressed you. Your firm conviction
that I called up the thunderstorms
doesn't count. That was a mistake. I think
my certain faith that the ball existed,
even when hidden behind the couch,
somehow gave you an inkling of my world.
In my world most things were hidden
behind something else. I called you "dog,"
I really wonder whether you perceived me
as a larger, noisier "dog"
or as something different, forever unknown,
which is what it is, existing in that attribute
it exists in, a whistle
through the nocturnal park one has got used to
returning to without actually knowing
what it is one is returning to. About you,
and who you were, I knew no more.
One might say, from this more objective
standpoint, we were two organisms. Two
of those places where the universe makes a knot
in itself, short-lived, complex structures
of proteins that have to complicate themselves
more and more in order to survive, until everything
breaks and turns simple once again, the knot
dissolved, the riddle gone. You were a question
asked of another question, nothing more,
and neither had the answer to the other.

[Y.L.S.]

Song of the Depths of the World, the Depths of the Eye, the Brevity of Life

The moral law within us. The starry sky above us.
But there's a starry sky beneath us too.
Galaxy upon galaxy deeper and deeper in an endless well
forgotten by our still medieval picture of the world
which still connects *sky* with *upward,*
and doesn't understand that if there are stars above,
there are stars beneath us too.
Glimmering in the depths. The moral law, too, must exist
under as well as over us, a law for those
falling endlessly, angels plunging in the comet
tails of their long hair, collapsing suns,
astronauts sleeping on board their ships,
Christians on board their cathedrals, sleeping
in their sepulchers, immense coffins
of marble and black basalt, journeying through
the maelstroms of those depths, everything journeying
toward the shore of resurrection
as through endless topological *involutions,*
the endless self-reproduction of the *set* into
itself, that is the shore we've never left.
Here we all sit, knights with greaves,
astronauts in protective helmets, and
Heraclitus, little old man bent over his acrid fire
of hard olive wood, all sitting by that same shore,
watching the minnows play, smelling the faintly acrid smell
of sunken timber, watching washhouse smoke
stretched out by the first autumn wind across the lake.
How quickly must the falling angels fall
in order to keep up with us, on our shore?
Does the heat of the fall cause them to glow? Or does the force
that's driving them? And is this moral law for
the endlessly falling, for the unfathomable depths
and for their more or less voluntary voyagers
on a par with the law for those forever rising?

Surely, much is concealed in the too dense foliage
of willows lining the roads in eastern Prussia;
many marl-pits are too shallow: there is a duty,
of course, but its negation exists in equal measure.
How right to relinquish self and speech! How
right to create a self where there was none,
how right to assert yourself, how right to feel desire.
Philosophers love to decide on the conditions
under which tenant farmers, day laborers, army privates,
beautifully liveried footmen in the rear
of light carriages should live; and above all,
I'd like to stress, what they should be capable of wanting:
from the duty of plowing without recompense
to the geraniums in the windows, which we,
that is to say the tenant farmers, should enjoy
viewing with disinterested interest. Exit Immanuel.
Bottomless snowstorms of galaxies under us,
insatiable desire within us, to all that can be desired,
to all this other darkness, which is
the other person, can offer us, of lust,
of secret knowledge, of seduction, and of hate.
Oh Sister Messalina! There is a needle point!
On this point we live, like angels!
(Perhaps we're angels, nonetheless, Sister Messalina?)
The great, enigmatic suns live and die,
kindled and extinguished in mysterious depths,
as far as the Well extends, and the dark
masses of gravitational collapse
plunge mightily into themselves at the border where
the narrow thread of time is stretched out
into a vast landscape, the room contracting
into a needle point. There we live
for all eternity, Oh Sister, under this Second Law,
Law for those falling endlessly, radiant,
filling forever this darkness with their glow.

Oh Heraclitus, the November day is short,
darkness comes across the lake, your fire begins
to show up more strongly in the darkness; yourself
you disappear among flickering shades. With ancient signs,
wonted constellations appear
in the sky, the November wind
moves the brittle reeds that move
with a drying sound. Across the western sky
a falling angel's track shows like a text.
Oh Master Heraclitus, it is time for us,
over the fire, to warm up a bowl.

[Y.L.S.]

Ballad of the Dogs

When Ibn Batutta, Arabian traveler,
physician, clear-eyed observer of the world,
born in Maghreb in the fourteenth century, came
to the city of Bulgar, he learnt about the Darkness.
This "Darkness" was a country, forty days' travel
further to the north. At the end of Ramadan,
when he broke his fast at sunset, he had barely time
to intone the night prayer before day
broke again. The birches glimmered whitely.
Ibn Batutta, Arabian traveler, journeyed
no further north than Bulgar. But the tales he heard
of the Darkness, and of the visits there, engrossed him.
This journey is made only by rich merchants,
who take hundreds of sledges with them, loaded
with food, drink and firewood, for the ground there
is covered with ice and no one can keep his balance.
Except the dogs: their claws take firm hold
of the eternal ice. No trees, no stones,
no huts can serve the traveler as landmarks.
Only those long-lived dogs are guides into
the Country of the Darkness, those old dogs
who have made the journey many times before.
They can cost a thousand dinars, or even more,
since for their knowledge there is no substitute.
At meals they are always served before the men:
otherwise the leading dog grows angry
and escapes, leaving its master to his fate.
In the great Darkness. After they have traveled
for forty days the merchants make a halt,
place their wares on the ground and return to their camp.
Returning on the following day they find
heaps of sable, ermine, miniver,
set down a little apart from their own pile.

If the merchant is content with this exchange
he takes the skins. If not, he leaves them there.
Then the inhabitants of the Darkness raise
their bid with more furs, or else take back
everything they laid out before, rejecting
the foreigners' goods. Such is the way they trade.
Ibn Batutta returned to Maghreb, and there
at a great age he died. But these dogs,
mute but sagacious, lacking the power of speech
and yet with a blind certainty that guides them
across wind-polished ice into the Darkness,
will never leave us in peace.
We speak, and what we say knows more than we do.
We think, and what we thought runs on before us,
as if that thought knew something we didn't know.
Messages travel through history, a code
masquerading as ideas
but meant for someone other than ourselves.
The history of ideas is not a knowledge of the mind.
And the dogs go on, with sure and swishing steps,
deeper into the Darkness.

[P.M.]

Ballad on the Stone Forest in Yunnan

In the province of Yunnan, two hundred and forty *li*
southwest of the city of Kun Ming where, still
on their solemn progress, junks are sailing
across the emerald green of Lake Tien Chi,
there's a vast forest of stone.
Travelers from early dynasties
speak of it with respect, even
with a sense of awe, as if they had seen
something forbidden, or
something which perhaps should not exist.
When Charlemagne was crowned in Rome,
when the deep-red color still shone new
from the pagoda of the Six Harmonies in Hang Chow,
far off at another river
this forest of stone was already the subject of ballads
by men who had wandered, or been carried in sedan chairs,
over the two high passes, along the three
lakes bordering the road, through gorges where,
in this year, the small green-uniformed soldiers
of the People's Liberation Army fight
the boiling radiators of clumsy lorries,
where men stripped to the waist haul timber logs
of superhuman size across two bicycles,
where black pigs are sniffing into potholes,
where cyclists ring their monotonous little bells
and men put a spring into their step to shoulder
burdens of dried corn and human manure,
in perpetual competition with their shadows,
and two by two the water buffaloes harrow
the meager dark-red fields, and sheaves of rice
have been laid down to be threshed by lorry wheels
just at the narrowest curve in the road.

It is this year: and we are still alive.
The forest is as vast as a whole county,
unimaginable. No wind has moved its trees,
these tall pillars of black basalt. The paths,
lined with ancient inscriptions, disappear
into sharp shadows: the facade of an organ
with fifty-meter pipes, which no one has played,
icicles which never melt, a text
whose characters reach to the very sky
and hide it, a somber text of stone
written long before man,
and no man shall retract it. What does it tell?
The path runs now through tunnels, now into daylight,
sharp light beats down on a stand of bamboo,
a woman of the Dai people, in singular clothes,
is hoeing a field the size of a sitting room,
right up to the roots of the pillars: round the next corner
we no longer believe that she existed, or
that she belonged to the same time as ourselves,
and our watches tick away, and show the same dead signs.
Deep inside the forest a river flows,
its black water washes against black pillars:
in that deep shadow, spiders
have spun huge webs. For ages they've been there,
the forest's guardians. Thinking alien thoughts.
I am forty-two years old, believe in nothing,
have tasted somewhat of life, without
bitterness and without hope: railway stations, airports
where the loudspeakers keep changing languages,
the great libraries where sunlight plays in the dust;
somewhat familiar with beauty: a drop of sweat
catching the light on a girl's silk-smooth belly,
thunderstorms over the lakes of Västmanland,
a mad dialogue of two flutes, *Adagio e piano*,
in a Trio Sonata of Bach, where nothing seems
to fit together and yet blends perfectly.

The Master Li Ko-jan, still alive in Peking,
painted a *Landscape on the River Li*
where stone and water merge into each other,
teaching us not to take stone too seriously,
not to take water too easily. Another Master,
who now lies dead in Peking, knew that the soft
can turn hard, the hard turn soft: in frost
keys snap off in locks, the warm wind breaks the dams.
So many clouds of dust have risen from the roads
of China! So many swords! So many deaths!
But this text in stone: someone wrote it,
someone for whom history didn't exist,
or maybe someone for whom everything was present,
immutable, everything in a single moment.
If you look at the stones, if you look into the stones,
close up, you can see a pattern there,
something that could be writing,
in the characters of a language before man.
Is the forest, then, a library? Who wrote it?
Who writes us? Could those novels be here
which we have not yet written? Epics
of those Long Marches which have not yet started?
Or is the whole forest about something else?
A text we are not permitted to read, message
from the extrahuman to the extrahuman,
who take no notice of us, and tell us
that we were meaningless? And therefore free?
Gods often speak that way, but not of us.
Now slanting shadows fall, the wind runs
through the bamboo, and above the river the western sky,
with a smell of smoke from the fields and houses, lifts
its yellow canopy. Who is writing us?

[P.M.]

The Stillness of the World Before Bach

There must have been a world before
the Trio Sonata in D, a world before the A minor Partita,
but what kind of a world?
A Europe of vast empty spaces, unresounding,
everywhere unawakened instruments
where the *Musical Offering,* the *Well-tempered Clavier*
never passed across the keys.
Isolated churches
where the soprano line of the *Passion*
never in helpless love twined round
the gentler movements of the flute,
broad soft landscapes
where nothing breaks the stillness
but old woodcutters' axes,
the healthy barking of strong dogs in winter
and, like a bell, skates biting into fresh ice;
the swallows whirring through summer air,
the shell resounding at the child's ear
and nowhere Bach nowhere Bach
the world in a skater's stillness before Bach.

[P.M.]

Eel and Well

In the province of Skåne there was a custom:
into their deep black wells they put
small eels from the sea.
And these eels spend their lives
imprisoned in the wells' deep blackness.
They keep the water crystal-clear and clean.
When sometimes the well-eel
is brought up in the bucket, white, frighteningly big,
blind, coiling in and out
of the riddles of its body, without knowledge,
everyone hurries to sink it back again.
Often I see myself
not just in the well-eel's place
but as both eel and well.
Imprisoned in myself, and yet this self
is something else: I'm there.
I wash it with my wriggling,
muddy, white-bellied presence in the dark.

[P.M.]

On Certain Evenings . . .

On certain evenings
the wall is warmer than the air.
Passing along this stone wall I feel
how it reflects the day
just as the great libraries
give out history
like a faint afterwarmth.

[P.M.]

Streams of Particles . . .

Streams of particles. Polarizations. Large magnetic fields that sweep like storms through enormous masses of dust and seek out all those grains that have a certain fiery gold brilliance.

Eddies that dance through black water, that rest in nothing and, swift as lightning, grow very hot.

Gases that cool just as swiftly and fall like hundreds of thousands of small, sharp, desolate drops.

The deepest layers of the soul look exactly the same as the universe in its totality.

Just so an ever-more-animated dream goes through the body of the big white dog.

[P.M.]

The Chinese Painter . . .

The Chinese painter P.
told me in Shanghai
about his childhood:
I used to watch timber
floating down the Wam Po.
I was eleven
and had to spend the night
in a kind of sentry box.
I was afraid of the spirits.
To protect me I had a cat.
To protect me against the spirits.
I tied a piece of string to the cat's tail
and tugged at it in the dark
when I felt lonely.
When the cat gave a wail
I felt less lonely.

[P.M.]

A Wind in Texas

Some days in April there's a peculiar southwest wind,
it starts in Ecuador, then crosses Mexico bringing
the jungle smell, the metallic note in the cries of the cardinal birds.
When it reaches southwest Texas, damp and warm,
the sleeping dogs lift up their heavy heads
on verandahs with their smell of rotting wood,
and the women, proud, red-haired, a little melancholic,
keep feeling at the laundry: when will it dry?

[P.M.]

The Decisive Battle . . .

The decisive battle is not
between power and power
but between the swift and the sluggish,
between mud and fire.
The swiftness of the poets
inside the circle of associations,
inside the fire. They must always be
one step ahead of censure
as the mongoose is always a fraction faster
than the rattlesnake.
What in the end destroys the *lager* state,
the guardian state, the police state
is the swiftness of the living man.
Like the best poets, or
the great mathematicians—an Abel, a Gödel, a Gauss—
the free man
is like the swallows whirring in June
around telegraph wires,
and always a little ahead of the premises.
Be in your own flight,
never wait for the footsteps on the staircase.

[P.M.]

Winter in a Westphalian Village

Someone up-ended a fine porcelain bowl
over the ponds and hills, over the trees.

Sometimes from above this bowl is lit,
outlines appear, a sketch of something. Yet vague.

The pond water isn't really frozen,
but, come to that, it isn't really water.

Interims: in the dusk
beams of a distant car tremble

like lights rising from the depth of the universe.
Too old to keep their wavelength.

Briefly at a bend the warming smell of a pigsty.
Two ducks take off, undaunted,

as if the underworld was full of birds.

[C.M.]

On the Speed of Swallows

And on a June day in Verona I saw a swallow,
it flew straight along a narrow street
between signs, trucks, laundry hung to dry,
as if none of these things really existed,
or as if the right way was apparent,
as a poem finds its way, or a waterfall,
so birds fall horizontally,
and still their fall is perfect.
Obstacles aren't always obstacles.
For some, the way through the world is evident.
Thus in Santa Helena Canyon the canyon swallow
falls, small and swirling, deeper and deeper into the darkness,
while the eagles, high up, gliding over Mexico's
hardly discernible donkey tracks, smugglers' paths,
tracks in the red stone, feel the evening rise up
as a faint warmth, out of the rock of the mesa,
one swallow resting, another faster,
into a darkness of wet rock, cliff and verdure.

Thus the same bird now falls into my poem,
into the poem, into me.
Thus we all fall inwards into ourselves,
out of an image, into an image.

And we aren't the eagle.
It waits till night falls
and veers away in another direction.

[C.M.]

Fragment

I've always had a liking for fragments.
The shred of papyrus, threadbare, brown
as an autumn leaf in the park in spring.
A philosopher quoted only once,
and then imperfectly, distorted,
by a very grudging patriarch,
who can't hide the golden glow
issuing from four words and a fifth
which is conjectural.

[C.M.]

La Salpêtrière: April 1980

Of Pinel, physician in chief at the clinic
during its classical period, it is said
that he took the manacles off the poor devils.

A commemorative portrait shows him:
a reasonable man, distinguished, peaceable, and kind,
surrounded by female patients;

also maenads, nymphs, priestesses
attending an unknown god of darkness,
who sends invisible snakes into their wombs.

Charcot and Freud are still far off.
Beside Pinel the blacksmith stands, amazed,
holding the pliers that broke the manacles.

What will happen next?
Locomotives, cathedrals of cast iron,
the contemporary machine gun.

This spring 1980, before the wars have begun,
the black cleaners in the Métro are on strike,
demanding to use the showers of the white cleaners.

Scraps of paper collect in indescribable drifts,
because this is the destiny of Europe,
and when the trains enter the illuminated stations

they drive before them clouds of loose pages,
papyri, ideograms, peace treaties, receipts,
like tiny snowstorms.

Fitful illumination. Fragments.
Flashes of light across half-obliterated signs,
and then, fast, back into the mother-darknesses.

[C.M.]

Looking at a Portrait of Lou Andreas-Salomé

The wide-awake cold gray in her eyes—
as if she had seen and understood

that life is large or small depending
on what we desire of it.

Her proud, queenly throat,
containing forever the sob—

sorrow at being a woman, being a body—
and all bodies are abandoned in the end.

Her proud hair catching the light.
Her very white skin, which knows

that skin is the border between
one hostile country and another.

[C.M.]

On All That Glides in the Air

My grave is still nowhere to be seen.
Thus I too glide,
resting, without knowing it.
In an ocean of air
gliding with all that glides,
living with all that lives,
resting with all that rests,
and perhaps, too, not knowing it,
dead with all that's dead.
There is no word for this.
It is a way to glide
"in the ocean of air" as old-fashioned balloonists did,
and this ocean of air is yourself.

Once in Texas at six in the morning,
swimming in the crystal water
of a very deep swimming pool,
intended actually for people who can dive,
my swimming suddenly became a gliding.
Looking down through the small goggle windows
at the marked black and white lanes,
from precisely the height that's fatal if you free-fall,
I could for a moment understand what it is:
to fall continuously, to be inside your fall
and still glide, carried by something invisible.
We see through the old painters and smile at them
and their childish trick of placing
far back in the picture very small birds,
gliding like reckless punctuation marks,
between earth and air, between light and shade,

between water and land, in short
the difference that comes between the differences,
the things of twilight that create the depth
which central perspective can't create alone.
So all mortals glide in the interior
of their own picture, somewhere in the twilight,
and for this gliding there is no name.

So also the signs glide over the white pages,
so the rooks glide over the snow, good times
over evil times,
so everything glides, stands as the angels stand
in an unthinkable motion,
and for the flight of the world there is no name.

[C.M.]

Flight of Cranes over Skåne at Dawn in April

The faint track of a bird is hard to trace,
and the wild cranes are few and far between.
Now comes the time to burn dead winter grass.

This dawn was like a happy woman, yes,
whose cry of pleasure rises pure and keen:
the faint track of a bird is hard to trace.

All birds are property of a hidden goddess
who taught them how to fly, fly and remain.
Now comes the time to burn dead winter grass.

A change occurs, the partner yields her place,
flight melting into light, he leads again:
the faint track of a bird is hard to trace.

Unfathomable moment. Flight, alas,
in vain—and stopping anywhere, in vain!
Now comes the time to burn dead winter grass.

And this white dawn, born blind, seemed to erase
my debt to death, secret as it had been.
The faint track of a bird is hard to trace:
now comes the time to burn dead winter grass.

[C.M.]

The Dogs

Their paws are firm and strong, they touch
the earth without a sound. Their noses,

cold and moist, know every smell
under the carpet of last year's leaves.

Many at once they come, and long
have come: none knows from where. They are swift.

They come in the daytime and at night,
and the evil they do, the good they do

cannot be told apart.

Their eyes are lead-gray ponds that formed
in a season before seasons began.

Into black waters lifeless petals
drop one by one. And leave no shadow

to shield that falling house's wall
where only the lizard, utterly still,

sits waiting till her moment comes.

On clear days we can hear their barking
lead from height to height, and then

it's lost for a time inside some valley
too deep for an echo to be born.

All we can do is guess their path,
sure only that they have our scent.

They sniff, they follow. They are our souls,
which once we left in silent forests.

And they will be on our tracks forever.
[P.M.]

The Starred Sky . . .

The starred sky, the fixed stare of the galaxies.
The universe *stubbornly* upholding enormous distances
against our just-as-eager strivings to see the world as small,
possible to survey, trafficable for signals and observations.
Quantum logic in physics and chemistry.
The same thing: matter's obstinate refusal to be
        anything but probabilities,
shadows that sweep over distant cliffs at sunset,
sudden gusts that run through a single aspen in the grove
and leave it almost still.
And our stubborn eager battle for a substance,
for particles, individualities, things that refuse to
        exist in the physical world.
This world of distances and shadows
and random leaps between the spectral lines,
this frighteningly still dance
is what I mean
by the world's stillness before Bach.
[P.M.]

The Birds

Canal Landscape with Ten Locks,
in the Dutch Manner

In
under the trees, the old trees that loyally
shade the ancient canal
with its lock-keepers' whitewashed houses,
its beehives, vines, its friendly dogs,
too often asleep, black water,
where quick as a lightning flash the swallows fly
one inch above the surface, never faltering,
fly close to the flowing black water
which hides forever the lost coin
which, in turn, on its way to the bottom,
gliding, will perpetually give back
the golden brilliance of the original light.
Into the ancient canal systems
of a strange country that is forever
hidden between the highways,
where the ten old houses of lock-keepers
still carry inscriptions on their walls,
where toward evening the old taverns open
to travelers from all ten townships,
who manage to sit together more or less at peace,
the dogs fall asleep again in the verdure,
the swallows glide and the vapors lift
from the waters, homely, like slow thoughts,
here we can talk again, here the birds fly still,
here nobody troubles us and if somebody does
it's only because he's nobody.
And the coin gliding to the bottom
is forever on its way.

                                    [C.M.]

Birdsong, Echo of the Original Paradise

In a garden in Belgium
I was woken up in the night
by the loud conversation
of blackbirds.
These voices that seem so sweetly to
imitate and return each other's mating call
and countercall,
modulation and iteration
all wanting to vary the signal
and still keep something recognizable
as in an old Provençal sestina,
coloratura and the echo of the singer himself, *sotto voce,*
and a primordial thought, so clear,
so foreign, so dry in all its heat
that it reveals, behind the singer,
the primordial reptile.
Because in some primordial garden
serpent and bird are one and the same.
Reptiles would sing, if they could, exactly like this,
exactly this is the sound from the Paradise garden.
If you could listen like this to the history of philosophy,
to its voices,
the clear voices and the obstinate ones,
the jocular ones that are elusive,
the insistent and wilfully repetitive voices,
the voices that dispute with vehemence
and the ones that are ironic and skeptical,
it would sound the same way:
an unintelligible quarrel in some garden
which turns before sunrise into song,
a very clear crystal, but not cold,
very hot, too hot to touch,
the echo, from a primordial garden, weakening,
the last glow of a primordial fire.

[C.M.]

Lot's Wife

It was not the case
that they did not warn me,
far from it, several times they told me
not to turn round.

Someone who can see the end
is not supposed to see the beginning,
yet I did and feel that my feet
are already too heavy.

It's turning to crystal now, the saltiness in me,
and there can't be more than seconds to go,
for some it's hard not to
hesitate at the last moment.

For some it's hard not to
look back with a cold eye
and stay forever at home in a town
which, for that reason, doesn't exist.

[C.M.]

Border Zone, Minefield, Snow East of Bebra

Only the barbed wire and glaring arc lamps
make this fresh snow distinct from any other.

All things are anguished at having
to exist in one form or another—

so many hawks glide over the mined snowy field,
not even small animals, one might suspect,

cross it unharmed. Catch and
pin have been so set

the lightest creature, even, would be blown to bits.
Out of blown clouds the full moon comes,

and the birds are gliding on and on, hungry still.
                                        [C.M.]

Placenta

This formless, lobed organ
which is, after birth, ejected.
Neither mother, nor child; neutral,
just as the innermost vacancy
inside profound insomnia
is a space entirely neutral.

Something is always there between
one ordinary condition and another,
neither this thing nor that.
Toward this in-between I have
a friendly feeling, sidelong,
a kinship, even.

It has the large, vacant, honest
face of the real world.

[C.M.]

The Cherry Tree

One night of sudden storm
the cherry tree fell
and when crest and trunk and twigs
had been pulled apart, set aside
the last cherries glowed
in the grass, random as they fell.
Nothing special about them,
no special taste or quality,
except they were the last.

[C.M.]

The Pansies

The pansies, small,
cruel and inquisitive
lion's faces coming out
in the garden in spring,
seem to say:
What spring? How long?
[C.M.]

Hunting Dogs

The delicacy of hunting dogs—
misconstrued, they are not tough
but sensitive, easily startled,
their real strength is the way
they stick to one thought.
[C.M.]

Comparison Between Insect Song and Bird Song

How strange to find in the same world
the song of birds,
which tells of love and sorrow so articulately,
of hesitation, rebellion, and contradiction,
and that older sound of insects,
which in its monotonous buzzing calm
seems to carry a much older thought,
a knowledge two or three steps
closer to creation.

They never discovered the negative.
[C.M.]

The Didapper

On clean clear autumn evenings
in small groups ahead of the motorboat.
Each disappearing, without fear or flurry,
only because
to disappear
is obviously its art.

Often I've wished
that I could follow it
in this second flight.
Does it see the surface
as a second sky?
How heavily do its wings beat now?

Does it think itself
the same bird in two disparate spaces?
One ruled by winds,
the other by cold deep swells.
The tree with leaves that quiver,
the long hair of seaweed

where the chill spring gushes upward.
How can it bring together
such different worlds in the one life?
Or does it think itself
two birds
which for an instant meet

at that mute whirling point on the water's surface?
[P.M.]

The Crows

Crows, black gyre
over a tree dead much too soon.
Band of gangsters gathering for black deeds,
or a party of revolutionaries
slipping one by one into the coffeehouse
in black, threadbare overcoats.
But also philosophers, sharp profiles,
deep pessimists: how shallow,
how prattling and coquettish magpies are
beside these big dark birds,
sinister shapes against the evening clouds.
Middle Ages, Battlefield, Gallows Hill:
what don't they know about mankind!
The crows, who always meet
in the naked tree
at the conclusion of each major tempest—
against clouds torn apart
like fleeing horsemen of some routed army—
meet in order seriously to discuss
the altered situation
which has now emerged.

[P.M.]

June Night

And back in the June night
the seagulls far out on wind-polished rock—
hermits between the waters,
holy men of fluff,
in ecstasy they scream toward the light,
the blind white light of the summer night,
scripture of light on white paper,
therefore frightening and illegible.

[C.M.]